GETTYSBURG

YOU ARE THERE

GETTYSBURG

YOU ARE THERE

ROBERT CLASBY

BURFORD
BOOKS

Printed in China.

10 9 8 7 6 5 4 3 2 1

Library of Congress Cataloging-in-Publication Data

Clasby, Robert

    Gettysburg: you are there/ Robert Clasby.

        p. cm.

    ISBN 1-58080-111-0

        1. Gettysburg, Battle of Gettysburg, Pa., 1863—Pictorial works.

        2. Gettysburg, Battle of Gettysburg, Pa., 1863. I. Title.

E475.53 .C63 2003

973.7'349'0222—dc21

2002151831

CONTENTS

INTRODUCTION

Gettysburg National Military Park holds an honored place on the list of solemn and sacred historic places in America. It is a list that includes a small wooden bridge over a river in Concord, Massachusetts, a dusty old mission in San Antonio, Texas, and a windblown hillside along the Little Big Horn River in South Dakota. For three days in July 1863, the town of Gettysburg and the fields, woods, and hills that surround it saw a combination of heroism and horror that forever marked the ground over which the battle was fought. The appearance of that battleground has changed dramatically in the 140 years since. Whole forests have grown up and modern roads, monuments, and buildings have transformed the landscape. The images in this book represent my attempt to show how the battle was fought over this unique ground. While I have removed many of the postbattle structures from view, it was not my desire to completely re-create the landscape of 1863. As a result, modern-day visitors to Gettysburg National Military Park will easily be able to recognize the locations shown in the book.

This book would not have been possible without the help of many people. First and foremost, I want to acknowledge the kindness and cooperation of the hundreds of men and women who reenact Civil War–era history throughout America. Their devotion to keeping our heritage alive was vital to the creation of this book. I also want to thank the National Park Service and the staff at Gettysburg National Military Park for all their patience and support. Finally, I will be forever grateful for the generosity and encouragement I received from family and friends. Thank you all.

Robert Clasby
February 2003

PRELUDE

*T*he hearse carrying Lieutenant General Thomas Jonathan "Stonewall" Jackson's body made its way through the Confederate capital city of Richmond, Virginia, pulled by eight plumed horses and flanked by a host of generals including James Longstreet, George Pickett, Richard Garnett, and Dick Ewell. Behind the hearse, Jackson's last horse, Superior, with reversed boots in its stirrups, led a long funeral procession, which included a carriage carrying his grieving widow, Anna, and an equally affected Jefferson Davis, the president of the Confederacy. Later on that day, May 12, 1863, twenty thousand citizens of Richmond and the surrounding country-side would file past the body as it lay in state at the Confederate House of Representatives. The grief would spread across the South as the news came in from Richmond. Stonewall Jackson was dead of his wounds. The wounds suffered when his own men mistakenly shot him in the murky, dark confusion that followed the spectacular flank attack he led at the battle of Chancellorsville. An attack that crumpled the right side of the Union line and sent a frazzled General "Fighting Joe" Hooker and the Army of the Potomac retreating back across the Rappahannock River. Many in the South, on hearing the news, refused to believe that Jackson was dead. They did not think it possible to kill him.

General Robert E. Lee knew that Jackson was gone. He, more than any other, knew what the loss meant, to himself, to his army, and to the whole southern cause. Since First Manassas, when Jackson and his men had stood firm under the Union onslaught on Henry House Hill, earning Jackson his celebrated nickname, through the Shenandoah Valley Campaign, the Seven Days, Second Manassas, Antietam, Fredericksburg, and finally Chancellorsville, the South and General Lee had been able to rely on Jackson and the men he led to march faster and hit harder than any other soldiers in the war. Now the South and "Bobbie" Lee would have to find a way to get by without him.

General Lee did not attend the funeral. It had been only a week since the victory by Lee's Army of Northern Virginia at Chancellorsville had thrown back another "On to Richmond" campaign by the Army of the Potomac. He was too occupied with keeping his ragged, ill-equipped, and hungry army intact to make the trek down to Richmond. The condition of the army and the entire Confederate cause did not leave Lee much time to grieve, even for Stonewall Jackson.

The remarkable victory at Chancellorsville over a much larger Union army had saved the Confederate capital once again and given Lee the initiative while the Army of the Potomac recovered and regrouped north of the river. While victory had bought time in the East, what was happening out west around Vicksburg, Mississippi, tempered any

GENERAL GEORGE G. MEADE, USA

celebration. General Ulysses S. Grant and his Army of the Tennessee, after weary months spent attacking impregnable bluffs, steaming up choked bayous, and digging worthless canals, had finally managed to get on dry land on the Vicksburg side of the Mississippi River. Grant's army was beating back the outnumbered Confederate forces in the region and would soon capture the Mississippi capital of Jackson before turning for the final push on Vicksburg. The loss of Vicksburg would open the entire Mississippi River to Federal control and cut off Arkansas, Louisiana, and Texas from the Confederacy, effectively taking them out of the war. Without the men and supplies these states could provide, the Confederate cause would be doomed, regardless of how many victories Lee and his army won in the East. Jefferson Davis, members of his cabinet, and several of his generals came up with various plans to reinforce the western armies and save Vicksburg, but all of them called for troops to be pulled away from Lee in Virginia. They reasoned that the Army of the Potomac would take a considerable amount of time to shake off the defeat at Chancellorsville and launch another campaign. Lee and his army should go on the defensive during the lull and would therefore be able to spare the troops needed in the West until Grant's army was crushed and Vicksburg relieved. General Lee disagreed. In the end, his opinion was what really mattered.

Robert E. Lee was the son of Revolutionary War hero "Light Horse Harry" Lee and part of an old aristocratic Virginia family. He had a distinguished military career before the war, graduating second in the West Point class of 1829, rising to Brevet Colonel during the Mexican War, and serving as superintendent of West Point for three years. When war broke out Lee was considered the finest soldier in the service and was offered command of the Union army, but turned it down. He could never take up arms against his beloved Virginia. He resigned his commission, joined the Confederate army as a general, and soon became Jefferson Davis's top military adviser. When General Joseph E. Johnston was wounded at the battle of Fair Oaks in May 1862, Lee took over command of the Army of Northern Virginia. His brilliant tactics, his willingness to risk everything for victory, and the devotion of his men had enabled his army to defeat every attempt by the always larger and better-supplied Army of the Potomac to capture Richmond. Throughout the long series of battles, Lee's reputation had grown to near-mythic stature in the South as well as in the North.

GENERAL ROBERT E. LEE, CSA

Lee had lost thirteen thousand men at Chancellorsville, along with the irreplaceable Stonewall Jackson. The Army of Northern Virginia was still badly outnumbered by the star-crossed Army of the Potomac, even though they had inflicted more than seventeen thousand casualties on that foe at Chancellorsville. The North could replace men and matériel at a rate the South could not hope to match. Lee felt that the threat from across the Rappahannock was much more immediate and dangerous than Davis and the others predicted. If he were forced to give up troops and the Army of the Potomac attacked, his army would lack the strength to maneuver and soon be pushed back into the Richmond defenses. With Union strength ever building while his army was left to wilt by attrition, Lee knew a siege of this kind could only end in defeat.

Lee had a plan of his own, one that fit with his aggressive character and could bring the South victory in the war within weeks. He would gather up his Army of Northern Virginia, reinforced with all available forces in Virginia and North Carolina, and march north across Maryland and into Pennsylvania. His hungry troops would reap supplies from the rich northern farms and towns untouched by war, capture Harrisburg, and threaten Baltimore and Philadelphia. The North would be thrown into a panic by such an invasion, and "Fighting Joe" Hooker and the Army of the Potomac would have to give chase. The Blue Army would have to come up fast by forced marches, and Lee would pick the time and place to attack the strung-out Union columns. Lee's army, concentrated, rested, and well fed, would pounce on the tired, disorganized Army of the Potomac and crush its corps one by one as they moved north. With the Army of the Potomac defeated, the road to Washington would be open and the North would have to sue for peace.

The plan was not without its risks. To march north would open the door for Joe Hooker's army to invest Richmond almost unopposed. Also, Lee and his army would be deep in enemy country when the final battle came. A defeat could mean the total annihilation of the Army of Northern Virginia—ending the war in weeks, but not the way Lee planned. Lee felt the risks were justified. He reasoned that Lincoln would not allow Hooker to move on Richmond and expose Washington to capture, reasoning that held true. As for defeat, that risk was always there. Lee's confidence in the men of the Army of Northern Virginia, who had defied the odds in victory after victory, was such that he knew if he brought them to battle on a favorable field, they would win. Perhaps he felt about his men like the people of the South felt about Jackson. They didn't think Stonewall could be killed. Lee didn't think his army could be defeated.

The respect and prestige that Lee had earned over the past year won the day. Lee's plan of northern invasion was approved by Jefferson Davis and his cabinet on May 16. That same day Grant and his army won the battle of Champion's Hill, which would push the Rebel troops defending Vicksburg back into the city's defenses and begin a long siege. Vicksburg and the men defending it would have to hold on as long as they could while Lee and his army took the fight into the heart of the Union. Lee rode north from Richmond on May 17 to prepare his army for invasion and the long gamble.

General Joe Hooker, the fourth and present commander of the Army of the Potomac, was not a popular man, especially with the powerful in Washington that included President Abraham Lincoln and his Commander-in-Chief, Major General Henry Halleck. Lincoln had reluctantly appointed Hooker to lead the army after General Ambrose Burnside had sent a good part of it to be slaughtered in front of the stone wall at the base of Marye's Heights overlooking Fredericksburg. Hooker was the most recent in a long line of failed Union generals to lead the Army of the Potomac. He knew that after he had let his superior force be flanked and defeated at Chancellorsville, his days in charge may be numbered. Despite this, he had returned to his brash ways in the days and weeks following the battle, having laid the blame for the defeat squarely on others, in particular General Oliver Howard's XI Corps, who had the misfortune to be on the right of the Union line when Jackson's men howled down upon their exposed flank. Hooker's refusal to take the blame may have been

GENERAL WINFIELD S. HANCOCK, USA

fortunate for the Union. It allowed him to dismiss the failure and get on with reorganizing what was left of his army. A smaller army to be sure, having shrunk, through casualties and the expiration of enlistments, from the 114,000 he took into battle at Chancellorsville down to 86,000 effectives. Hooker had retreated to the vicinity of Falmouth, north of the Rappahannock, and was in the process of trying to figure out what to do next when he received reports that Lee's army was on the move heading north and west.

Lee had started reorganizing the Army of Northern Virginia for an offensive even before he had received permission from Davis and the cabinet to attack the North. Instead of the two wings under Longstreet and Jackson as in the past, it would now have three corps. The I Corps would be commanded by General James Longstreet, Lee's "Old War Horse" who had served him so solidly throughout the war. The II Corps would go to Richard "Dick" Ewell, who had served ably under Jackson and was just coming back to the army after almost a year of recovering from losing a leg at the battle of Groveton. Ewell was a brave and dependable commander, but he was used to the firm hand of Jackson to guide him. The III Corps would go to General Ambrose P. Hill, an impulsive and aggressive general who had also served under Jackson. Hill could be counted on to attack the Federals whether they outnumbered him or not, but he suffered from occasional poor health that could flare up from stress brought on by impending battle. To lead his cavalry, Lee had promoted James Ewell Brown "Jeb" Stuart to lieutenant general and increased his strength to ten thousand horsemen. Flamboyant and skilled, Stuart had ridden rings around Federal cavalry throughout the war. Even more critically, he had provided accurate and prompt information about the dispositions and movements of enemy troops that had enabled Lee to consistently confound his adversaries. Lee started his movement on June 3 by sending Longstreet and the I Corps northwest toward the Blue Ridge Mountains. Ewell and his II Corps soon followed, heading west into the Shenandoah Valley. A. P. Hill and his men stayed in place for a few days in Fredericksburg to block any quick Union strike across the Rappahannock.

GENERAL JAMES LONGSTREET, CSA

The Army of the Potomac had its observation balloons up and noticed the empty Confederate camps almost immediately. Hooker knew that Lee was on the move and wanted to attack the blocking force of A. P. Hill's corps right away and deal with the rest of Lee's army later. That idea was vetoed immediately by Lincoln and Halleck, who demanded Hooker keep his army between Lee's marching columns and Washington. They suggested attacking the moving corps of the Army of Northern Virginia as they were strung out on the roads. This rankled Hooker, who felt the grip from above denying him his chance to take advantage of this opportunity to open the road to Richmond. He complied, however, getting his army started to shadow Lee northward. His famous temper was starting to boil, though, and his patience with taking orders from a civilian president was growing thin.

Jeb Stuart took advantage of his higher position and increased command by throwing a party. The focus of this party would be a grand review of his troops by important civilians and would include all the pomp Stuart could muster, which was considerable. It would even include a mock cavalry charge against artillery firing blank but loud and smoky charges. Stuart held the review on June 5 at Brandy Station, and it was a grand spectacle that was followed by a ball for officers and ladies. Stuart enjoyed it so much that he held the review again when General Lee arrived on June 8 on his way north with the infantry. It was a memorable event enjoyed by all, but took its toll on horses and men who, after all, were supposed to be preparing for a climactic invasion into Pennsylvania instead of riding around impressing fashionably dressed ladies and gentlemen. Meanwhile, General Hooker was breaking camp to move his army north and was desperate to know where Lee was going. He sent Major General Alfred Pleasanton out with three divisions of Union cavalry to find out. In the early-morning hours of June 9, while most of Stuart's command was getting some much-needed sleep after the festivities of the past four days, one of Pleasanton's divisions under Brigadier General John Buford splashed across the Rappahannock at the lightly defended Beverly Ford. Brushing aside the Rebel pickets, Buford and his horsemen penetrated deep into the surprised Rebel cavalry camp. Stuart and his men rallied quickly, however, and Buford's outnumbered Union cavalry were fought to a standstill and finally pushed back out of the camp. Just when he thought he had things well in hand, Stuart was again surprised by Pleasanton's other two cavalry divisions, who had come up by way of Kelly's Ford and circled around into his rear. A wild melee followed as first Union and then Rebel cavalry charged and countercharged. The

Union cavalry, much maligned throughout the early years of the war, fought toe-to-toe with Stuart's command for several hours before retiring back across the river. Stuart was left with possession of the field and the right to claim victory in the largest cavalry battle of the war, the battle of Brandy Station. It had been a close thing, though, and Stuart had to suffer the sting of being taken completely by surprise in his own camp. He and his troopers would also have to contend with a much more confident Federal cavalry for the rest of the war.

Lee didn't let the big cavalry show at Brandy Station slow down his advance. He had concentrated around Culpeper, west of the cavalry battle, and quickly had his three corps on the road toward the Shenandoah Valley. Ewell's II Corps led the way through Chester Gap, followed by A. P. Hill and the III Corps. Longstreet's I Corps headed north and crossed into the valley by way of Ashby's Gap. Ewell's corps were in the lead on June 15 as the Confederate army advanced on Winchester. Ewell was a changed man since he had rejoined the army. During his convalescence he had married a rich widow and found religion. The profane and irascible man who had done so well under Jackson was now quiet and devout. Many of his men worried that his new demeanor did not bode well for his ability to lead one of Lee's corps. Ewell quickly had an opportunity to dispel those fears. A Union garrison of six thousand soldiers under the command of General Robert Milroy was garrisoning Winchester. Milroy wanted to put up a fight despite being warned to retire by Washington. Ewell silenced his critics by aggressively attacking from three sides and swallowing up Milroy's entire command in a fight that became known as the second battle of Winchester. The easy success of the battle cleared the way north through the valley. Lee's army of seventy-seven thousand men was on the march north to Pennsylvania, shielded from view by the Blue Ridge Mountains.

GENERAL JOHN F. REYNOLDS, USA

The Federal cavalry continued to try to penetrate far enough into the valley to divine Lee's whereabouts and fought a series of battles with Stuart's troopers in Middleburg, Aldie, and—on June 21—Upperville in the attempt. They managed to push their way up to the gaps, but couldn't force their way through. Lee had slipped away, and Hooker was left to ponder his intentions. Discouraged once again by Lincoln in a second request to cut loose from the Army of Northern Virginia and advance immediately on Richmond, Hooker resumed the march north toward a crossing of the Potomac.

Jeb Stuart, still recovering from the damage done to his reputation by the surprise at Brandy Station, had accomplished his first duty of keeping Lee's infantry screened from the probes of Federal cavalry. He now requested of Lee that he be allowed to leave two of his brigades to continue the screen, while he and three of his best brigades rode south and east, clear around Hooker's army, disrupting supply lines, cutting communications, and harassing any Union advance. Stuart had gained great acclaim earlier in the war by just such a maneuver around Union general McClellan's forces in the Peninsular Campaign. A repeat performance would clear the bitter taste of Brandy Station and once again bring him praise in the southern newspapers, an important thing to Stuart. He felt he could accomplish the raid in a few days, in time to link up with Ewell's corps north of the Potomac and resume shielding the infantry as they advanced. It was a bold proposal, but Lee's command style was to give his subordinates wide latitude in how they accomplished his orders. Lee gave his consent, but warned Stuart that he must be sure to rejoin the army in time to screen the advance into Pennsylvania. Stuart took what he interpreted as permission and set off on his ride on June 25. He would have to ride hard. The men in the van of Ewell's column were already marching on the roads north and east of Chambersburg, Pennsylvania.

The Army of the Potomac was also on the move. Hooker had marched his lead divisions up to the Potomac at Edward's Ferry in good order by June 25, and the entire army was across the river on its way to Frederick, Maryland, by the twenty-sixth. If Hooker did not know what Lee and his army were up to behind the Blue Ridge Mountains, Lee was even less aware of what Hooker was doing to the southeast. Counting on the long tradition of slow methodical movement by the Army of the Potomac,

MAJ. GEN. GEORGE E. PICKETT, CSA

Lee assumed Hooker was still breaking camp south of the Potomac. He would have been quite surprised to learn that by June 27 Hooker had concentrated most of his army around Frederick in a position to seriously threaten Lee's invasion force, strung out as it was from the lower Shenandoah Valley north as far as Carlisle and east as far as York. Hooker had done an admirable job of moving his bulky army fast, but he was still trading disagreeable telegrams with Lincoln and Halleck in Washington. Their disputes finally came to a head when Hooker requested the Union garrison at Harpers Ferry be withdrawn and added to his army. A seemingly practical request, as the garrison had been bypassed by Lee and Harpers Ferry had proved indefensible earlier in the war, surrounded as it was by high commanding hills. When the request was denied, an exasperated "Fighting Joe" pressed his point by submitting his resignation. Lincoln and Halleck finished the squabbles by accepting it and sending a courier by special train to wake General George Gordon Meade and inform him that he was now in command of the Army of the Potomac.

Meade was a competent general who had risen to command the V Corps. His bulging eyes and unpredictable outbursts of temper had earned him the nickname "the old snapping turtle" in the army. Being appointed the Army of the Potomac's latest commanding general in the midst of a desperate campaign to throw back a Confederate invasion didn't make him any less testy. But he took on the burden as the professional soldier he was, and got right to work taking control of what was now his army.

The Army of the Potomac woke up in their bivouacs around Frederick, Maryland, on the morning of June 28, 1863, to find themselves under a new commander who was unfamiliar to most of them. There was some grumbling among the troops about the change and the selection of Meade, but this army had been through so many battles under so many generals that they just boiled their coffee and went on with their duties with the fatalistic attitude of all veteran soldiers. They would march hard and suffer the thirsty, terrifying, brutal work of battle when the time came. As for Meade's ability to deal with Robert E. Lee, they had learned not to expect much help from generals.

The men of the Union army would have been pleased to know that their long march of the past few days had already upset the plans of the Confederate forces they would soon face, in particular Jeb Stuart and the five thousand troopers he had brought along on his ride. The northern army's march up to Frederick had clogged the roads Stuart had planned to use, and he was forced to swing much farther south to get around the Army of the Potomac. In fact, on the morning of the fourth day since his departure, June 28, when he expected to be far to the north closing in on a link-up with Ewell and the II Corps in Pennsylvania, he and his horsemen were eighty miles south of Ewell, finally crossing the Potomac River at Rowser's Ford. Most of the day after crossing the river was taken up in the pursuit and capture of 125 Federal wagons loaded with supplies just north of Washington. They were a valuable prize too tempting for Stuart to pass up, but now his progress north to his prime assignment would be slowed even more by his newly acquired wagon train. His troopers and their mounts were tiring fast, and Stuart would have to push them even harder over the next few days to catch up with the infantry.

As far as Robert E. Lee was concerned, Stuart and his brigades might as well have been out west fighting indians for all the good his best cavalry was doing him. June 28 found him in Chambersburg with his army spread out north, east, and south. Ewell had divided his corps, with one half under division commander Jubal Early sent east through the passes of South Mountain, past the small road-junction town of Gettysburg and on to York. Ewell led the other half north to Carlisle and was marching on Harrisburg, the capital of Pennsylvania, with nothing but nervous state militia to stop him. Hill and the III Corps had reached Chambersburg on the twenty-seventh and were now gathered just east of the South Mountains near Cashtown. Longstreet and the I Corps were on the road south of Chambersburg and coming up fast. The cavalry Stuart had left behind were not able to supply Lee with the information he needed, and he was desperate to know where Stuart was and, more importantly, where the Army of the Potomac was. He soon found out about

COL. JOSHUA CHAMBERLAIN, USA

the latter, but not by any word from Stuart. A spy, sent by Jefferson Davis, brought news to Lee that the Army of the Potomac, now under the command of George Meade, was gathered in and around Frederick. This was a shock to Lee, who found it hard to believe that this movement of the enemy could have taken place without some warning from Stuart. He had to act on the information quickly. To ignore it would be to expose his widely dispersed army to piecemeal destruction. Lee sent orders calling Ewell and his command back to Chambersburg or Gettysburg, as circumstances might dictate, but soon changed the location to Gettysburg for a link-up with Hill and the III Corps, who would be coming down the Chambersburg Pike from the west. Longstreet and the I Corps were ordered to force-march north and east to complete the concentration of the Army of Northern Virginia near the little college town of Gettysburg, Pennsylvania.

General George Meade had some important decisions to make, and he needed all the information he could gather to make them. To get it, he had ordered his cavalry brigades to fan out north of Frederick and find out where Lee's army was and where it was going. On the morning of June 30, two of these brigades—led by General John Buford, the hard-fighting, West Point–trained Kentuckian who had started the fight at Brandy Station—rode into Gettysburg and learned that a large column of Rebels had come through town headed east a few days before. He also heard that as many as twenty thousand more, A. P. Hill's entire corps, were eight miles west in Cashtown and headed his way. Buford sent a patrol west to confirm this and that patrol immediately ran into part of Hill's Corps, more than two thousand Confederates under James Johnston Pettigrew, already gathering on Seminary Ridge on the western outskirts of Gettysburg. Pettigrew and his brigade weren't looking to start anything. In fact, they were just on their way to Gettysburg to conduct a reconnaissance in force and see if any supplies had been missed by Jubal Early's men when they passed through town a few days before. Pettigrew had been issued orders by his division commander, General Harry Heth, to avoid getting himself into a fight. Lee had made it clear all down the chain of command that a battle was to be avoided until the army could concentrate. So when it became clear that Gettysburg was occupied by a sizable body of Union cavalry, Pettigrew withdrew his men from the ridge and headed back west to Cashtown. The cavalry patrol returned with the news that there were indeed considerable numbers of Rebels west of town. Buford realized that Gettysburg and his two thousand troopers were in between large parts of the Rebel army and that holding the town where all the surrounding roads converged could be vital. He also knew that to hold it he would need help, and lots of it, very fast. He sent a courier to Meade at his headquarters in Taneytown, Maryland, laying out the situation as he saw it. He also sent word to General John Reynolds, commander of the Union I Corps, who had his men camped six miles south. Reynolds was considered one of the finest officers in the Union army; it was rumored that he had turned down the job of leading the Army of the Potomac when Lincoln had offered it to him after Chancellorsville. Apparently, the control from above that had so rankled Joe Hooker and the other leaders of the army before him was unacceptable to John Reynolds. If Meade decided to send Buford support and make a fight at Gettysburg, Reynolds and his I Corps were good men to have come in first. Once the couriers had been sent, Buford got busy organizing his defense on the ridges just west of town. He would stay there as long as he could.

Meade had devised a plan in the two days that he had been in command, and it didn't include a battle near Gettysburg. He had intended to find Lee and his army and lure them into attacking him in prepared positions behind Pipe Creek near Union Mills, Maryland. He had even issued orders to his seven infantry corps commanders to fall back on that line once they bumped into Lee's army. When word came in from Buford that he held good ground at Gettysburg and needed large numbers of infantry to hold it, Meade reluctantly decided to send his army north, but kept his option to fall back on the Pipe Creek line open. He sent word to Reynolds to take command of the III and XI Corps, along with his I Corps, and move north in support of Buford. That reluctant decision would end up starting the chain of events that pulled more and more forces from both sides into battle at Gettysburg.

Harry Heth was mindful of Lee's orders not to bring on a general engagement, but he did not like it when he heard that Pettigrew and his brigade had been turned back from Gettysburg by mere cavalry. He believed that the Union troopers encountered in Gettysburg were just a scouting party and would have ridden well clear if Pettigrew had just pushed a little. Infantry was not supposed to be stopped by cavalry, especially in his command. He took the news of the encounter to A. P. Hill and requested that he be allowed to take his whole division east into Gettysburg and finish the job the next morning. Hill, always keen to encourage an aggressive subordinate, approved the idea.

DAY ONE *July 1, 1863*

H eth had his division on the Chambersburg Pike marching east toward Gettysburg by sunup on July 1. A few miles west of town, Heth's men chased off some Federal cavalry pickets, who fired a few long-range shots and galloped east to alert Buford that a long column of gray infantry was on the way. The land west of Gettysburg rolls out from town in a series of low ridges that run north and south with broad, shallow valleys in between. On one of these ridges, called Herr's Ridge after a nearby tavern, Heth's division encountered their first stiff opposition. Buford had set up a line of defense, a few squadrons under Colonel William Gamble, on the ridge. Heth put part of his infantry in line and pushed the badly outnumbered Federal cavalry off Herr's Ridge. The troopers

Brigadier General John Buford's dismounted cavalry attempt to hold McPherson Ridge west of Gettysburg. The Union troopers, with the aid of their rapid-firing Sharp's carbines, held off the attack of two brigades from Harry Heth's Confederate division just long enough for John Reynolds's I Corp to arrive and secure the ridge. This view is north of the Chambersburg Pike looking northwest across Willoughby Run toward Herr's Ridge in the distance.

This 1863 photograph shows the woods south of the McPherson Barn where General John Reynolds was killed while ordering the "Iron Brigade" into battle on the morning of the first day's fight. The cupola of the Lutheran seminary, which was used as an observation point for both sides during the battle, can be seen in the distance.

gave way grudgingly, falling back in a skirmish line that harassed and slowed the Rebel advance toward the next high ground on the way to Gettysburg, McPherson Ridge. Buford had set up his main line of defense on McPherson Ridge, straddling the Chambersburg Pike north and south. When Heth came over the crest of Herr's Ridge, he saw Buford's dismounted cavalry and a few field guns waiting to contest his move into Gettysburg. His skirmishers out front were already testing this line, and it soon became clear that Buford and his men had no intention of being brushed out of the way. Buford's cavalry were armed with Sharp's carbines, breech-loading weapons that allowed a much more rapid rate of fire than the standard infantry shoulder arm. Heth watched his forward units pull back under a hot fire from the cavalry's carbines. Heth would have to give a harder push to convince this Federal cavalry to hand over the road to Gettysburg. Fortunately for him, he had brought along plenty of men to push with. He deployed a brigade under Joseph Davis north of the pike and one under James Archer to the south. Almost three thousand men formed in line facing east and started their advance down the broad slope of Herr's Ridge, across a little stream at the bottom of the valley called Willoughby Run, and up toward the waiting Union troopers. John Buford, from a perch atop the cupola of a Lutheran seminary on Seminary Ridge, just east of McPherson Ridge, watched as Heth's main battle line formed and advanced on his thin line of cavalry. This was the time when, in the accepted tactics of the day, his cavalry should give one or two last volleys at the advancing infantry and quickly mount up and get clear before the weight of the Rebel infantry line overwhelmed them. But Buford was not inclined to give any ground that day. He had selected a good defensive position atop the ridge, and behind him lay a town he intended to keep. He knew Reynolds and the I Corps were on the way north to help. He had sent a courier earlier in the day letting them know a fight was on and to hurry up. His men and their fast-firing Sharp's carbines on McPherson Ridge had to buy him a little more time. Time would be expensive that morning.

The Confederate infantry had marched into range, and their lines were erupting in the smoke and flame of packed volleys. Buford's men were firing back fast, their carbines so hot now that hands burned and curses flew. Men in both lines fell dead and wounded as Buford watched his line of troopers edge back east along the crest of the ridge. It was almost 10 A.M. and the sun had burned off the morning clouds. It was already hot in the cupola. Sweat soaked Buford's uniform. He knew his brigades needed help fast or he would have to order them off that ridge if he wanted to have a command left at the end of the day. Just then, John Reynolds yelled up a greeting from below.

Reynolds had ridden ahead of his I Corps, now on the march north up the Emmitsburg Road, to see what all the noise was about just west of Gettysburg. The view from Seminary Ridge told him all he needed to know about what the cavalry was facing to the west. Buford told him of reports of more enemy infantry on the way in from the north and east. Reynolds decided that the ground Buford and his men had held on to that morning was worth keeping. He immediately sent aides riding south to hurry his men along while he rode out with Buford to study the ground. The I Corps weren't far away, just south of Gettysburg and coming on fast. Reynolds then rode south himself to the Emmitsburg Road to meet his men and ordered the lead division under General James Wadsworth to leave the road and cut across the fields southwest of town to go directly to the fight. The lead brigade of Wadsworth's division, under Lysander Cutler, came up on McPherson Ridge north of the pike and struck the left side of the Rebel line just as the exhausted Union cavalry was giving way. To the south of the pike, Reynolds directed the other half of Wadsworth's division, the Iron Brigade, a renowned outfit made up of midwesterners who wore distinctive high black hats, to attack through a small tangle of woods on top of the ridge. Archer's Rebel brigade was just then coming into the west side of the woods to flank the evaporating Federal cavalry line. As Reynolds urged the running "Black Hat Boys" into the fight, he tumbled from his horse, shot in the head and killed by one of the thousands of Minié balls searing through the air atop McPherson Ridge that morning. The commander of all of the

Dead Union soldiers lie scattered over the fields west of Gettysburg. Their missing shoes show that scavenging Confederate troops held the field after the fighting.

Union forces engaged at or on the way to Gettysburg that day was gone, just as the battle was getting started. Command of the I Corps would pass to General Abner Doubleday. Reynolds had made the decision to fight it out at Gettysburg. It would be left to others to see if his decision was sound. The Iron Brigade would do their part. Crashing into the woods, they blasted Archer's brigade, who had come in expecting to face outnumbered cavalry and instead run into one of the best infantry brigades in the Army of the Potomac. Still, Archer's men put up a hard fight until they were flanked and forced out of the woods. Then they fled. Piling up behind a rail fence near Willoughby Run on their flight back to Herr's Ridge, many were taken prisoner, including General Archer himself.

The fight was not going as well for Cutler and his brigade north of the pike. There were no woods to provide cover, and when the three regiments of Cutler's brigade appeared, Davis and his men were ready. The opposing lines blasted each other from close range, causing horrific casualties on both sides. Cutler's men began to fall back, and the northern part of the Union line bent back east as the Rebels bore down on their flank from the northwest. An unfinished railroad cut, running just north and parallel to the Chambersburg Pike, seemed to provide perfect cover and a safe route for Davis's men as they flanked the Union position. They crowded into the cut and began to march past the Union line in perfect safety. Cutler's men, bolstered by a regiment of the Iron Brigade that had been held in reserve, realized what was happening and charged north from the Chambersburg Pike to cut them off. The Railroad Cut deepened as it led east, and Davis's men found themselves unable to oppose the charge because the cut was too deep to fire out of. Union infantry swarmed forward and fired down into the packed mass of Rebel troops from atop the steep sides of the cut while calling for surrender. Those of Davis's men who could ran back west through a gauntlet of rifle fire to safety on Herr's Ridge.

Many were shot in the attempt to flee, and more than two hundred others threw down their rifles and surrendered to the jubilant Yankee troops.

Other than the artillery banging away at each other from the opposing ridges, the morning's fight was over as Archer's and Davis's battered brigades climbed back up to the relative safety of Herr's Ridge. The stiff resistance of Buford's cavalry and the timely arrival of the I Corps under Reynolds had thrown back Heth's attack with heavy losses on both sides. The noontime sun shone hot on thousands more soldiers from the two armies who were marching in on the roads that converged at Gettysburg. When and where they would arrive would play a crucial role in determining who held the field at the end of the day.

On the roads north of Gettysburg, marching south fast, were Ewell and the Rebel II Corps. Already headed toward Gettysburg after Lee's previous order to concentrate in that direction, Ewell had received the news that Hill's III Corps were heavily engaged west of town. This put his corps in an excellent position to come down hard on the right rear flank of the Union line, which was thus far totally undefended. The first division of Ewell's Corps to reach the scene, under General Robert Rodes, came in down the Mummasburg Road from the northwest and gathered on Oak Hill, a prominence northwest of Gettysburg where McPherson Ridge and Seminary Ridge converged. Rodes, a veteran officer who had led his division in Jackson's flank attack at Chancellorsville, saw a great opportunity to repeat that success by attacking the exposed right flank of Doubleday's west-facing line on McPherson Ridge. The opportunity would not last long, however. Looking down into Gettysburg from the top of Oak Hill, he could see long columns of Yankee troops moving north through town. He ordered an immediate attack, sending in his regiments piecemeal over ground he hadn't taken the time to reconnoiter. His men ran headlong into massed Union infantry hidden behind a long stone wall. The Federals rose and fired from close

THE UNFINISHED RAILROAD CUT

JULY 1, 11:15 A.M.

Two Confederate regiments from Joseph Davis's brigade attempted to flank the Union line north of the Chambersburg Pike by marching down an unfinished railroad cut. The tactic turned into a disaster for Davis's men when Union regiments charged the cut from the Chambersburg Pike. The cut was too deep for the Rebels to fire out of and turned into a deadly trap. More than two hundred Confederates were killed or captured, and the rest beat a hasty retreat back to Herr's Ridge. The view is looking west from the north bank of the cut.

range, scything down row after row of the surprised Alabamans in the van of the attack. Rodes fed more of his men into the battle as they came up, only to see them suffer equally under the withering fire from the stone wall before retiring back to Oak Hill.

The men Rodes had seen coming through Gettysburg, which had spurred him to rush his disastrous attack, were from the Union XI Corps, commanded by Major General Oliver Howard.

Howard had marched his corps, made up mostly of German immigrants and frequently referred to as "Dutchmen" in the slang of the day, to Gettysburg that morning after a summons from Reynolds. Shortly before arriving, he had received two pieces of bad news. The first was that Reynolds was dead and that he was now the senior officer on the field. The second was that a whole host of Confederates were about to arrive from the north. Howard, who had lost an arm at the battle of Seven Pines, would now be called upon to take control of the battle and counter this new Confederate threat. His men of the XI Corps, who had lost their confidence after their rout at Chancellorsville, would have to rush north and hold back the oncoming Rebel tide. Neither Howard nor his corps were very well suited for their jobs. Howard passed command of the XI Corps to General Carl Schurz, ordering him to take three divisions and form an east-to-west line north of Gettysburg, closing up with the flank of the I Corps on McPherson Ridge. Howard held one division in reserve and had them start digging entrenchments on a rise just south of town called Cemetery Hill. There Howard would place his headquarters and direct the rest of the day's fight.

Schurz's divisions rushed through Gettysburg and formed their line on the broad open farmland north of town, linking up with the I Corps to the west. The right side of the line was anchored on a little knoll alongside the Harrisburg Road, where Brigadier General

This 1880s photograph shows the Railroad Cut where the men of Davis's Confederate brigade became trapped on the morning of July 1. The railroad tracks had not yet been laid at the time of the battle.

Federal dead from the first day's fight are testament to the appalling casualties both sides suffered when the two armies collided west and north of Gettysburg.

Francis Barlow had pushed forward his division. To the east of what would forever after be called Barlow's Knoll, there was wooded ground, rapidly filling with concealed gray-clad soldiers. Once again, just as at Chancellorsville, the XI Corps' right flank was "in the air."

General Robert E. Lee had arrived at the battle, and what he found dismayed him. After learning of the bloody repulse of two brigades from Heth's division earlier in the day, he stood atop Herr's Ridge with A. P. Hill and watched Rodes's men brutally broken up in their attack from Oak Hill. Heth was there, too, embarrassed by his morning failure and aware that he had brought on a battle Lee had hoped to delay until after his army was all together. Heth, having re-formed his entire seven-thousand-man division in line along the crest of Herr's Ridge, requested permission to renew his attack to support Rodes. Lee turned him down. He did not have his army concentrated as he had hoped, and it was apparent from his view from the ridge that the Union corps confronting him were being heavily reinforced from the south. With still no news from Stuart, he had no idea whether he might be facing the entire Army of the Potomac with half of his own army still scattered west and north. Lee had decided to break off the battle until he could get his army concentrated and prepared. Then all hell broke loose out by the Harrisburg Road.

Jubal Early and the wing of Ewell's II Corps that had made it as far east as York before being recalled had marched down the Harrisburg Road and found themselves in the perfect position at the perfect time to attack the exposed right flank of the Union XI Corps. Early had formed his troops in a solid wall astride the Harrisburg Road and sent them crashing into Barlow's division, defending the knoll. Lee hadn't become an almost mythical military figure by letting such opportunities pass by. He immediately reversed his decision and ordered Hill to attack east with everything he had. For once Lee had the advantage, not only in position but also in numbers, twenty-five thousand men on the

THE XI CORPS ARE FLANKED NORTHEAST OF GETTYSBURG
JULY 1, 3 P.M

The men of Jubal Early's Confederate division, after overwhelming the Union division under Francis Barlow, arrive on the flank of the Union XI Corps. Just as at Chancellorsville, the XI Corps' flank is "in the air" and the results are the same. The XI Corps were soon routed and sent running for their lives southwest into the streets of Gettysburg. The view is looking west from the vicinity of the Harrisburg Road northeast of Gettysburg. Oak Hill can be seen rising in the distance.

attack against sixteen thousand unentrenched defenders. To the east, Barlow's men fought desperately but were soon surrounded on three sides and forced to retreat from the knoll, leaving behind many dead and a badly wounded Barlow. The rest of the jumpy XI Corps' line were hit hard from the flank and rear and were rolled back and sent fleeing south into the streets of Gettysburg. On McPherson Ridge the outnumbered I Corps fought furiously as Heth's division, including two fresh Rebel brigades, poured across Willoughby Run. The Iron Brigade, taking and inflicting hundreds of casualties, were pushed out of the woods they had won that morning and off the crest of McPherson Ridge, falling back east to Seminary Ridge. A brigade under Colonel Roy Stone held on for a while near the McPherson Farm until almost surrounded, then fought bitterly as they retreated back to Seminary Ridge, leaving a trail of torn blue-clad bodies behind. The remnants of the I Corps made another stand around the Lutheran seminary, but A. P. Hill sent in another division under Dorsey Pender, and the overwhelming Confederate attack again broke through and pushed them back into the streets of Gettysburg, already crowded with men from the routed XI Corps. The Confederate corps of Hill and Ewell, wild with the momentum of victory, streamed into town after them from the west and north. What followed was a wild, violent melee through the streets of once sleepy Gettysburg. The unfamiliar thoroughfares were clogged with men of both armies fighting for intersections, dodging through backyards, and climbing over fences. Panicked artillery horse teams plowed through dazed regiments as men fought from house to house. Units lost all semblance of organization in the maze of smoke-shrouded buildings; officers of both sides had little control over the battle in the town. The onslaught of Rebels scooped up thousands of Yankee prisoners and sent the remnants of the Union I and XI Corps running out of the south side of town to take refuge on Cemetery Hill where Howard had his headquarters. The reserve division held back by Howard that morning had fortified Cemetery Hill, and their position was backed by a long line of artillery pointed north. The surviving men of the I and XI Corps quickly took up positions facing west and north along the slopes of the hill to prepare to beat off the next Confederate attack. That attack would not come, at least not on this day. It was now around four o'clock in the afternoon, and the victorious southern divisions were just about as shot up, disorganized, and exhausted as the men they had just pushed through town. General Ewell had launched the attack from the northeast without orders from Lee, and while it had all worked out gloriously he still did not have permission to bring on a full-scale engagement. When the battle through the streets of Gettysburg petered out, Lee did send a courier to Ewell asking him to continue the attack and try to take Cemetery Hill if he thought such an attack stood a good chance of success. Ewell didn't think it did, at least not yet. The Federals held a strong position on Cemetery Hill, and Ewell's corps would have to be disentangled from the town and formed for an attack. A fresh division under Edward Johnson were on the way to Gettysburg, and Ewell felt it was crucial that they participate in any assault. All of this would take time, time the battered northern army on Cemetery Hill would use to fortify and organize. Ewell sent word to Lee that to attack the hill he would need support from A. P. Hill and the III Corps from the west. When Lee approached Hill with the request the sickly general begged off, knowing how badly mauled most of his corps were from their full day of battle. Lee sent word back that if Ewell's corps were going to take Cemetery Hill, they would have to do it alone. A mile to the east of Cemetery Hill there was a higher, heavily wooded rise known as Culp's Hill. It appeared to be as yet unoccupied by anyone, and Ewell's gaze shifted that way. Instead of charging head-on into the cannon on Cemetery Hill, he contemplated the effect it would have if he could get some men and

McPHERSON BARN

JULY 1, 3:45 P.M.

In a last attempt to hold back the afternoon Confederate attack on McPherson Ridge, a small brigade, made up entirely of Pennsylvanians under Colonel Roy Stone, makes a stand east of McPherson Barn until almost cut off by the overwhelming Rebel attack. Stone's brigade made a fighting retreat back to Seminary Ridge and finally was pushed into the town of Gettysburg with the rest of the I Corps. The view is looking southwest from the vicinity of the Railroad Cut.

artillery up on those heights. Plunging fire from Culp's Hill would make the Union position indefensible and force them to retreat. It was a sound idea, but unfortunately for the southern army, Ewell did not act on it quickly.

Another man had his eyes on Culp's Hill, and he wasn't the kind to hesitate. Major General Winfield Scott Hancock had arrived on Cemetery Hill with orders directly from Meade, who was still back in Taneytown, to take command of the field and determine whether the army should stand and fight at Gettysburg. Hancock had only recently risen to command of the Union II Corps and was junior in rank to General Howard, but he was the kind of professional soldier whose very presence inspired confidence on a battlefield. After a brief, uncomfortable conference with Howard, who was reluctant to accept that he had been usurped, Hancock plunged into organizing the defense of Cemetery Hill, riding about the hill directing new arrivals into line and bringing the dazed survivors of the day's fight back to life. He saw the threat posed by Culp's Hill and immediately ordered Wadsworth to take what was left of his battered division and occupy the heights. Wadsworth protested that his men were all used up from the long day's fight, but Hancock insisted and sent him on his way. Major General Henry Slocum and his XII Corps began to arrive, coming north up the Baltimore Pike. Hancock put one of Slocum's divisions in reserve and placed the other so as to extend the I Corps line south down the west face of Cemetery Ridge to the base of a thinly treed rocky hill known locally as Little Round Top. A solid defensive position was coming together and the morale of the Union soldiers was starting to rise, thanks in large part to the work of Hancock.

It was close to six o'clock before Ewell got around to ordering Johnson and his still-arriving division to head up what Ewell believed were the unoccupied slopes of Culp's Hill. He did not push Johnson to hurry and did not give any orders on what to do if Johnson ran into opposition. After directing Johnson, Ewell rode off west to consult with General Lee. It took Johnson another hour to bring all his men up and get them in line. When they finally started up the thickly wooded, rocky slopes of Culp's Hill, they were met with concentrated volleys from Wadsworth's division, who had been on the hill for more than an hour piling logs and rocks into the beginnings of stout fortifications. With no orders to launch a full-scale attack with his whole division on such a well-defended position, Johnson pulled his men back and went into camp for the night. By the time Ewell returned, the sun

McPherson Farm in a picture taken a few weeks after the battle. The large barn on the left still stands on the ridge that saw much of the first day's fighting. The house and outbuildings on the right no longer exist.

had set and there was no time to order an attack before full dark. Ewell's decision not to follow up on his corps' rout of the Union right flank by quickly launching an attack on Cemetery or Culp's Hill before the end of the first day's battle disappointed many of his own officers. They felt that the Army of Northern Virginia's best chance for total victory that day had been squandered when Ewell hesitated. After all, they knew "Stonewall" Jackson would have been leading these troops if he had not been shot down at Chancellorsville. Ewell was finding it hard to follow a legend.

The brief clash when Johnson's men brushed up against the Culp's Hill defenders effectively ended the fighting for the day. Lee's army went into camp, bivouacking west of Cemetery Hill along Seminary Ridge, north in and around Gettysburg and east along Rock Creek facing Culp's Hill. Lee had every reason to be encouraged by the day's battle. His army had routed the better part of two Union corps, gained the road hub of Gettysburg, and taken four thousand prisoners. Two of his three corps were in position on the field, and Longstreet's I Corps were on the way from Chambersburg. In fact, Longstreet himself had arrived at Lee's headquarters to witness the final retreat of the Federal forces as they fled to Cemetery Hill. Lee, once it became clear that Ewell was not going to push on through to the heights, decided to renew the attack the next day when all his forces would be on hand except one of Longstreet's divisions under George Pickett, who were at the rear of his column. Longstreet argued for a different course. He saw a great opportunity, now that Meade's army had been located, beaten, and condensed south of Gettysburg, to swing the Army of Northern Virginia south then east and interpose it between the Army of the Potomac and Washington. Once there, they could find a good defensive position and repeat the slaughter of the Union army as at Fredericksburg, but on an even grander scale. Longstreet reasoned that Meade would have no choice but to attack given the panic such a maneuver would stir up in Washington. Lee was unconvinced. Slipping away from an unfinished battle went against his way of thinking. He had come north to destroy the Army of the Potomac, and his army had gotten a good start on the job that day. Stuart and his best cavalry were still missing, making maneuver in the face of the enemy even riskier than it normally was. Lee was determined to attack and defeat the Army of the Potomac on the hills and fields south of Gettysburg. He would spend most of that night and next morning planning how to do it.

George Meade finally arrived on Cemetery Hill in the early-morning hours of July 2 after a long ride up from Taneytown. Having sent his army north to support Buford's appeal for help, he had given up control on where and when his battle with Lee would start. First Buford, then Reynolds, Doubleday, Howard, and finally Hancock had made the decisions that brought on and expanded the first day's fight. Now Meade would take control of the battle and make the decisions that might determine the course of the entire war. That burden weighed heavily on him as he surveyed the ground around Cemetery Hill. It was a strong position. Even by moonlight he could see that Hancock had placed the troops in a dominating line running from the heights of Culp's Hill, west to Cemetery Hill, and then jogging sharply south, as the ground fell away, in a straight line to Little Round Top. It was a defensive alignment that would forever after be known as the Fishhook, due to its shape when represented on a map. Meade's first objective after surveying the terrain was to gather his army and hold this position. The depleted I and XI Corps had been reinforced by Slocum's XII Corps and most of Dan Sickles's III Corps, but more than half of Meade's ninety-three-thousand-man army was still on the road marching north. Judging from the galaxy of smoldering campfires Meade observed off to the west and north, he would need all of them to hold on to Cemetery Hill.

DAY TWO *July 2, 1863*

L ee awoke from a few hours of sleep before sunrise on July 2 with the same determination to assault the Union line he had had the night before, but unsure exactly where to place his troops to start the attack. He was still hampered by a lack of information brought on by Stuart's continued absence. A consultation with Ewell that morning had ruled out a full-scale attack on the left. Culp's Hill was too well suited for defense, and the Yankee forces had continued to fortify it. Cemetery Hill, in the center, was by this time bristling with men and guns secure behind stone walls. Lee decided to attack on the right, using two of Longstreet's divisions under John Bell Hood and Lafayette McLaws, along with a III Corps division under Richard Anderson that

OVERLEAF
DEVIL'S DEN
JULY 2, 4:30 P.M.

On the left flank of the III Corps line, a Union brigade under J. H. Hobart Ward stubbornly clings to Houck's Ridge and the jumble of huge boulders on its southern end known as Devil's Den. Some of the fiercest fighting of the entire battle took place amid this brutal terrain. Repeated attacks by regiments from Hood's division finally pushed Ward and his men out of Devil's Den and off Houck's Ridge for good. The view is looking west toward Houck's Ridge from a boulder-strewn area just east of Devil's Den that came to be known as the Slaughter Pen.

An 1880s photograph of the north face of Devil's Den.

hadn't taken part in the previous day's fighting. That would give Longstreet, who would command the assault force, close to twenty thousand men to send plowing into the Union left flank and roll the blue line up to Cemetery Hill. Lee's problem, as the sun came up, was that he did not know exactly where that Union left flank was or how many men were defending it. Before sending Longstreet and the three divisions south to position for the attack, he had to have that information. Riders were sent out to survey the ground, and by the time they returned it was midmorning. They reported that the Federal line ended just north of Little Round Top. In fact, both of the dominating hills to the south of Cemetery Hill—Little Round Top and heavily wooded Big Round Top farther south—were completely unoccupied. This was good news to Lee, who ordered Longstreet to place his divisions in line perpendicular to the Emmitsburg Road west of the Round Tops and advance northeast along the road into the Union flank. Lee also sent orders to Ewell, telling him to make a demonstration against Culp's Hill when he heard the sound of Longstreet's assault to prevent Meade from stripping the right side of his line to support his left flank. Once again Longstreet protested. The news that the left side of Army of the Potomac was wide open made it clear to him that his original suggestion to swing the Army of Northern Virginia south and east was now even more sound. If Lee insisted on attacking that day without maneuvering the entire army south, didn't it make more sense to attack directly east, seize the Round Tops, and cut Meade's supply line to Washington? Lee would have none of it. The army he intended to crush that day was on Cemetery Hill; attacking into a vacuum south of that objective was not acceptable. Lee gave Longstreet his orders again to march his three divisions south, undetected if possible, and begin the attack when they were in position across the Emmitsburg Road. A sullen Longstreet set out to comply.

Over on Cemetery Hill, Meade was starting to feel more confident. The morning respite while Lee got a feel for the ground and planned his assault had given the Army of the Potomac the time to come up to near full strength. The rest of Sickles's III Corps had arrived along with Hancock's II Corps and George Sykes's V Corps, bringing Meade's strength up to almost seventy thousand men. Only John Sedgwick's VI Corps were still on the road. Meade had placed Hancock and his men south along Cemetery Ridge and assigned Sickles's men to extend the line farther south reaching down to Little Round Top. The security of numbers had boosted Meade's morale to the extent that he started to consider going on the offensive. He saw Culp's Hill and its dominating height as a good location to launch an attack against Ewell's men across Rock Creek. But caution prevailed. Meade, only a few days in command and on the wrong end of the previous day's battle, decided to wait and see what Robert E. Lee had in mind.

James Longstreet, had he known of Meade's momentary urge to attack, would have strongly encouraged him to do so. Longstreet, more than most of the officers in the Civil War, was aware of how futile frontal attacks against prepared positions were in that era, given the accuracy and range of the rifled guns and Minié balls that both armies used. If Meade would have done the Army of Northern Virginia the favor of beating Lee to the punch and attacking on July 2, Longstreet would have been happy to have called off his attack and joined in the slaughter of the advancing Federal lines. As it was, he had Lee's orders and would carry them out. But he would take his time. As he saw it, time might give his absent third division under Pickett a chance to complete their march in from Chambersburg and add another five thousand men to his attack. A delay might also give George Meade enough time to bolster his courage and order his army to charge out from their lines. Lee grew impatient and rode to Longstreet's camp to inquire about the delay

Dead Confederate soldiers in Devil's Den.

and learned that Longstreet was awaiting an Alabama Brigade that was just marching in. It was noon before Longstreet ordered his men to break camp and assemble. The long column of men who would make up the attack, led by Lafayette McLaws's division, traveled south along Herr's Ridge toward the positions Lee had designated for the attack, but soon came to a halt. A treeless expanse of the ridge lay ahead, and McLaws saw that if the column marched over it they could be clearly observed from the crest of Little Round

A dead Confederate sharpshooter lies behind a breastwork in Devil's Den.

Top where a Federal signal flag could be seen wigwagging messages. If Meade learned of the impending attack and shifted forces south to meet it, Longstreet knew that the likelihood of a bloody repulse was high. Secrecy had to be maintained, even if it meant more delay. He ordered a countermarch back north up the ridge and brought the column south farther to the east, screened by the woods of Seminary Ridge. It was a hot day, and the long column became even more strung out as the movement turned into a thirsty, sweat-soaked ordeal. Finally, several hours after setting out, Longstreet had his divisions in the woods north and south of the Emmitsburg Road due west of the Round Tops, close to the jump-off point for the attack. While the men sorted themselves out into lines of battle, artillery fire started to fall among their ranks. The fire came from cannon stationed in an orchard of peach trees alongside the Emmitsburg Road to the northeast. Further inspection found that the cannon were protected by thick lines of Union infantry, forming a salient north and east of the Peach Orchard. The Union left flank had moved dramatically since Lee had formulated his plans many hours before, thanks to a politically appointed Union general named Dan Sickles.

Sickles had received command of the III Corps in the Army of the Potomac through political connections and a friendship with Joe Hooker. He had little in the way of military training and was looked on with disdain by most of the West Point—trained officers in the army, including George Meade. With Hooker gone, his relationship with Meade was one of mutual contempt. Sickles had arrived at Cemetery Hill with his III Corps early that morning and Meade had put them in line, facing west, south of Hancock's II Corps. Sickles didn't like the ground. Cemetery Hill dropped off in elevation as it ran south toward Little Round Top, and by the time it got to Sickles's assigned position there was little in the way of elevation left. His left flank was anchored by the imposing heights of

Little Round Top, but he felt he didn't have enough men to stretch his line effectively from where the II Corps ended all the way south to occupy the hill. He also observed out to his front a rise of mostly bare ground, except for a small peach orchard, that seemed to command his position. Enemy artillery stationed near the Peach Orchard could fire down upon his men. Sickles thought it would be much better if he took his corps west and occupied the rise around the Peach Orchard before the Rebels did. He sent a message to Meade outlining his concerns and requesting permission to make the move. Meade dismissed the request. The placement of Sickles's III Corps was part of the unbroken chain of defense that Meade had organized for his army, and they would have to stay where they were or disrupt everything. Sickles would just have to deal with local terrain conditions as best he could. This didn't sit well with Dan Sickles. He requested that Meade come personally and take a look. Meade, burdened with the demands of command at his headquarters in the Leister House on Cemetery Hill, declined the invitation and again sent back word that Sickles should stay where he was. As the day wore on, while Longstreet and his men were marching and countermarching through the afternoon, Sickles became more and more agitated about his position. He finally went personally to see Meade and requested that he be allowed to move his corps forward to the high ground. Meade again denied the request, but sent his chief of artillery, Henry Hunt, back with Sickles to look over the ground. Hunt didn't have the authority to order a change even if he agreed that the III Corps should move forward. A frustrated Sickles sent a regiment to do a reconnaissance of the woods to the west of the Peach Orchard. The regiment ran into long columns of Rebels just on the other side of the woods line and had to retreat quickly. They had stumbled into the right flank of the Army of Northern Virginia, extending its line south along Seminary Ridge. This news convinced Sickles that he was not only in danger of being attacked from the high ground to his front, but might also be flanked by southern troops moving around his left, screened by the Round Tops—which he had, amazingly, still failed to occupy. Sickles was done asking permission. He ordered his entire ten-thousand-man corps into line and had them march forward to positions facing west along the Emmitsburg Road running south to the Peach Orchard. There, the new line turned sharply east and extended through a forest called Rose's Woods to Houck's Ridge just west of Little Round Top, ending at a jumble of huge, oddly shaped boulders known as Devil's Den. In an effort to improve his position, Sickles had unlinked his corps from the rest of the army, sent it forward almost a mile to form a vulnerable salient at the Peach Orchard, and lengthened his line such that his brigades had been stretched thin all along his front. Just before four o'clock in the afternoon, Meade had finally found the time to ride out and inspect Sickles's original position. Horrified to find the III Corps gone, he rode out to the Peach Orchard to confront Sickles. He got there just in time to witness the start of Longstreet's attack.

The appearance of Sickles's corps in their advanced location caused almost as much consternation among Longstreet and his division commanders as it did George Meade. The Union III Corps was now positioned directly across the line of attack up the Emmitsburg Road that Lee had ordered Longstreet to take much earlier in the day. As John Bell Hood positioned his division on the far right of the Confederate line crossing the Emmitsburg Road, they came under fire from a row of Federal cannon in the Peach Orchard. Hood sent out scouts to see what Union forces would be on the right flank of his northeast attack up the Emmitsburg Road, and they came back to report that there wasn't a Yankee soldier to be found clear to the south slopes of Little Round Top. Hood immediately sent a courier to Longstreet requesting he change the direction of his attack and head straight east toward the Round Tops, bypassing the new Federal position established by Sickles.

THE CHARGE OF THE 20TH MAINE JULY 2, 5:30 P.M.

On the wooded southeast slope of Little Round Top, Colonel Joshua Chamberlain and his 20th Maine Regiment occupied the extreme left flank of the entire Union army. After withstanding repeated assaults by the 15th and 47th Alabama Regiments, Chamberlain's men were nearly out of ammunition and about to be overrun. Chamberlain, knowing that retreat would mean disaster for the Union, ordered a bayonet charge that crushed the surprised and exhausted Alabamans. The Union left flank had been saved. The view is looking southeast from just inside the 20th Maine's breastworks.

Union breastworks on Little Round Top.

Confederate soldiers killed while attacking through the woods south of Little Round Top.

Once there, Hood and his men could wheel north into the unprotected rear of the Union army and, quite likely, send it into rout. When this request reached Longstreet it was almost four o'clock in the afternoon. He had already pressured Lee to send the army south of Cemetery Ridge and been turned down repeatedly. To delay the attack further, as would be necessary to shift the lines to head east, and change Lee's plan of attack was more than Longstreet could do. Longstreet sent back a reply ordering Hood to proceed with the attack, guiding on the Emmitsburg Road to the northeast. Longstreet's attack would be *en echelon* from right to left. Hood's division, on the far right of the Confederate line and now positioned north and south of the Emmitsburg Road in Biesecker's Woods, would attack first, followed by McLaws's division, in line hidden in Pitzer's Woods to the west of the Peach Orchard. Finally, Anderson's division would attack east from the middle of Seminary Ridge. The hope was that the mounting pressure on the left flank of the Union line would force them to send reinforcements garnered from the center and right. When the twenty-thousand-man attack rolled north, the depleted blue line would be too thin to hold. Hood was displeased when Longstreet's message arrived denying his request to attack east. He felt that Longstreet didn't understand the situation to his front. At just after four o'clock, he ordered his men forward, telling them to guide on the Round Tops. He was taking it upon himself to capture the heights. His line emerged from the cover of the woods and was soon taken under fire by batteries on Houck's Ridge. The batteries were part of a brigade under Brigadier General J. H. Hobart Ward that held the left flank of Sickles's corps anchored on Houck's Ridge and Devil's Den. The artillery fire exploded around the surging Confederate line, taking the first casualties of the attack. Hood, leading his men across the fields, was hit in the arm by a fragment of an exploding shell and carried to the rear. He was out of the battle and would lose the use of his mangled arm forever. The command of the division passed to General Evander Law, who continued to lead most of the division east into the thick woods west of Big Round Top. Two regiments on the left of the line veered north to confront the defenders of Houck's Ridge head-on, creating a gap in the line. Law shifted two regiments from the far right to fill the gap and sent them to attack directly into Devil's Den. The rest of the brigade kept heading east, slowed only by a skirmish line made up of a crack green-uniformed regiment called Berdan's Sharpshooters who would pick off a few men and retreat. Law's lines bulled their way through and headed up and over undefended Big Round Top and then north toward Little Round Top.

On the crest of Little Round Top stood Brigadier General Gouverneur Warren, Meade's chief of engineers. Warren had ridden down Cemetery Hill with Meade when he came to make the inspection of Sickles's original line. Meade, after finding out Sickles had pushed his corps forward, sent Warren to see what the situation was on Little Round Top. Surely Sickles had not left it undefended. But he had, as Warren was quick to find out when he reached the summit and found only a small signal team stationed on the hill. Warren then watched as most of Law's men were swallowed up by the thick cover to the southwest near Big Round Top. He realized that the Union army was about to be flanked, and he was standing on the last defensive position available to save it. He needed to find troops and bring them up fast. Already the first Confederate wave could be seen crashing into Houck's Ridge, a few hundred yards to the west across a little stream called Plum Run.

The fight Warren was watching was the left end of Law's line trying to push Ward's brigade out of Devil's Den and off Houck's Ridge. The fighting was brutal. The Rebel regiments attacked and were blown back by canister fired from the batteries atop the ridge. They regrouped and charged again. Ward's men were pushed back and then, after getting reinforcements from Regis De Trobriand's brigade to the northwest, charged forward and

Dead Confederate soldiers litter the swampy, boulder-strewn ground east of Devil's Den that became known as the Slaughter Pen.

reclaimed the ridge. The maze of boulders that made up Devil's Den saw some of the worst fighting. Hundreds of men swung rifle butts and lunged with bayonets among the rocks on Ward's extreme left in what would become known as the Slaughter Pen. Another gray brigade under Henry L. Benning rolled into the fight and surged around both sides of Houck's Ridge. Ward kept pushing fresh regiments pulled from other parts of the line forward, only to have them chewed up by Confederate volleys. The south end of Dan Sickles's salient was giving way.

General Warren hadn't waited to see how the fight around Houck's Ridge turned out. He knew that even if Ward's brigade held off the attack, losing Little Round Top to the Confederate regiments now concealed in the woods to the south would bring disaster to Ward's brigade and the rest of the Army of the Potomac. He sent for the first troops who could be found to try to save the position. The V Corps under George Sykes were gathered in reserve northeast of Little Round Top. One of Sykes's brigades under Colonel Strong Vincent, a twenty-six-year-old graduate of Harvard, was marching west to support the III Corps when a winded aide rode up and implored Vincent to change course to Little Round Top. Vincent, realizing the importance of holding the heights, ignored his current orders and sent his regiments south to defend the rocky hill. They had barely arrived and started organizing in a line facing south when his regiments on the southwest slope were hit by Law's men coming northeast through the saddle between the Round Tops. They beat off one assault but were overwhelmed by the next. Vincent himself led the desperate effort to hold the line but was shot dead by the onrushing Confederates. Just when it appeared that nothing could keep the Rebels from taking the heights, the 140th New York, a regiment found and sent by Warren himself, crested Little Round Top and threw themselves down the hill, breaking the Rebel charge. On the southeast slope the carnage continued. The

20th Maine, a regiment led by Colonel Joshua Lawrence Chamberlain, a rhetoric professor at Bowdoin College before answering the call to war, held the left flank of Vincent's improvised line. This meant that the men from Maine found themselves anchoring the extreme left flank of the entire Union army. If they were pushed aside, the way would be clear for the Confederates to swarm into the Union rear, creating the rout Hood had envisioned. The smoke and thunder of battle rolled east toward the 20th Maine until out of the trees to their front came a rush of screaming Rebels. Two regiments from Alabama under the command of Colonel William Oates surged up the hill, only to be forced back under a maelstrom of fire. Oates sent his men up again, this time farther east to flank the 20th Maine's position. Again they were repulsed, but only after Chamberlain bent the left side of his line back to refuse the flank. By now many of the Twentieth's men were nearly out of ammunition and had to resort to digging into their dead comrades' cartridge boxes. Again the relentless Alabamans attacked, scrambling up the hill and fighting their way into the crumbling blue line. Chamberlain saw his men falling away, and with them any chance for Union victory in the battle. Chamberlain did the only thing he could think of. He ordered a charge. The thinned ranks on the left side of the 20th Maine line jumped to their feet and stormed down the hill with bayonets thrust forward. The surprised Alabamans, who had been either marching or attacking all that hot day, had fought to their limit. The charging Yankees rolled them back like a swinging door from left to right as more and more of Chamberlain's line joined in. The exhausted Confederates fled. Those who could ran to safety back over Big Round Top. Many, tired and beaten, threw down their rifles and surrendered.

Heroic charges by the 140th New York and the 20th Maine had saved Little Round Top and with it the Union left. It would take more than that to save Dan Sickles and his III

LITTLE ROUND TOP AND THE VALLEY OF DEATH
JULY 2, EARLY EVENING

Little Round Top, a rocky hill whose western face had been mostly cleared of trees, dominated the left flank of the Union army. A little stream call Plum Run ran through the valley separating Little Round Top and Houck's Ridge. The view shows regiments from Hood's Confederate division driving the remnants of Ward's Union brigade through the "Valley of Death" and assaulting the heights. Union reinforcements quickly gathered by General Gouverneur Warren can be seen defending the top of the hill. The heavily wooded slope of Big Round Top rises on the right. The view is looking east from Houck's Ridge.

Photograph of Little Round Top taken a few days after the battle.

Corps. Ward's brigade, along with several regiments sent to reinforce him, had finally been pushed off Houck's Ridge and thrown back to Plum Run. They made a doomed stand in the little valley between Little Round Top and Houck's Ridge, forever after known as the Valley of Death, but were soon sent fleeing back to the southern slopes of Cemetery Ridge.

An 1863 photograph of breastworks on Little Round Top with Big Round Top rising in the distance.

Northwest of Houck's Ridge, De Trobriand's brigade occupied a line that ran along a stone wall on the southern border of a field of wheat and extended west through Rose's Woods toward the Peach Orchard. Longstreet was continuing Lee's plan of sending in his forces one after another from right to left, and as the attack rolled north it struck De Trobiand's brigade hard. A gray brigade under George "Tige" Anderson hit the defenders of the stone wall in front of the Wheatfield and sent them reeling back. De Trobriand called desperately back for reinforcements and got them in the form of two brigades from Sykes's V Corps. They came in at the quick and helped take back the wall and sustain the line. The attack rolled north as another southern brigade under Joseph Kershaw came in and struck the Union line between Rose's Woods and the Peach Orchard. This push had weight behind it and the Federal line was thrown back, isolating De Trobriand's command in the Wheatfield on the left. Caught in a pocket with Kershaw's men threatening to cut them off, De Trobriand's men gave up the wall and desperately fought their way back out across the Wheatfield to a patch of trees known as Trostle's Wood. There they made a stand, and a vicious firefight ensued while urgent messages were sent back to Meade for help. Help was already on the way, but Meade was forced to strip his forces on Cemetery Ridge to provide it. One of Hancock's II Corps divisions under John Caldwell was sent south down Cemetery Ridge to bolster the cracking Union line. The first of Caldwell's brigades to arrive pushed the Confederates back to the southern side of the Wheatfield and stood in a long line across from Anderson's Georgians, delivering and taking close-range volleys. The Wheatfield was littered with dead and dying men; a thick pall of smoke hung over the field and woods. With the Rebel advance halted, Caldwell sent in the rest of his force, led by the Irish Brigade, who had gained fame for their attack on the sunken road at Antietam. Following their bright green flag, the Irish Brigade led a line of two thousand men who

THE WHEATFIELD JULY 2, 6:15 P.M.

A small rocky field of wheat northwest of Houck's Ridge became a killing ground as Longstreet's attack rolled north. The battle lines surged back and forth across the field as both sides fed reinforcements into the fight. With no cover to protect them, exhausted men from Georgia and New York slammed volleys into each other amid the carnage. The view is from the east side of the Wheatfield looking west.

plunged into the stunned Confederates. The charge pushed the spent Rebels back and regained the stone wall and Rose's Woods. The Union line east of the Peach Orchard had held at the cost of thousands of casualties, but the Rebel attack again rolled on as Longstreet fed in more brigades from McLaws's division.

Just west of the Peach Orchard across the Emmitsburg Road and a wide field, the brigade of William Barksdale, a former fire-breathing secessionist congressman from Mississippi,

Confederate dead awaiting burial near the Wheatfield.

waited under cover of the woods to join the fight. Barksdale was champing at the bit, pleading with Longstreet to let his men join in the attack. Longstreet, seeing the Union line sweep forward and retake their lost positions, finally let Barksdale go. His fifteen hundred men emerged from the trees in a tightly packed front and marched toward the salient of the Union line. The Peach Orchard was surrounded by artillery who had been wreaking havoc on the flanks of the Rebels attacking the Wheatfield and Rose's Woods. Many of the

Bodies strewn across the Wheatfield.

guns had been firing furiously for an hour and were low on ammunition and not positioned to fire west into Barksdale's assault. Marching quickly across the field, Barksdale's men weathered a Union volley and then charged over the Emmitsburg Road into the tangle of Federal artillery and infantry. A confused, violent struggle among the peach trees ended with Barksdale's men pouring through the line, capturing guns and Yankees, and sending blue refugees streaming back east. Sickles had no reserve to call on to save his pierced line, and his corps started to collapse north and east from the Peach Orchard. Another Rebel brigade under William Wofford, accompanied by Longstreet himself, came in behind Barksdale's men and widened the gap, turning north and attacking the flank of Andrew Humphrey's Union division, arrayed facing west along the Emmitsburg Road. Humphrey tried to hold but was forced into a fighting retreat when his line was also hit from the west by the first brigades of Richard Anderson's division to join in the attack. To the east, the exhausted men of Caldwell's Union division, whose charge had just finished reestablishing the Union line, turned to see Barksdale's and Wofford's screaming men surging across their rear. The real fear of being cut off sent Caldwell's men and the remnants of Sickles's corps running back toward Cemetery Ridge. The rout was on as more of Anderson's division poured across the Emmitsburg Road to support the attack.

Sickles's corps and the thousands of troops sent to support them were pushed east toward the undefended portion of Cemetery Ridge that Sickles had abandoned earlier in the day. Some would re-form and fire into the oncoming Rebel tide before continuing the retreat, while others had lost all order and simply ran east completely out of the battle. Hancock, looking out on the now unopposed Confederate brigades forming for the final push over Cemetery Ridge, knew men had to be found to plug the gap or the battle was lost. His corps had already been depleted by Caldwell's departure earlier in the day. Now he looked around for men to throw in the way of the oncoming rush of Confederates. He found them in George Willard's brigade, whom he personally led south to confront Barksdale's final push. The fresh Union brigade fixed bayonets, formed across the path of the tiring Rebels, and forced them back, riddling Barksdale's body with Minié balls in the process. He would die in agony a Union prisoner two days later. A fifteen-hundred-man brigade of Alabamans under Cadmus Wilcox were the next threat to confront Hancock and the yawning gap in the Union line. Hancock rode down the ridge desperately searching for support. All he found was the 262 men of the 1st Minnesota. This small regiment had spent the battle guarding the reserve artillery on Cemetery Ridge. Hancock ordered them out to attack the oncoming Alabamans. Their commander, Colonel William Colvill, Jr., ordered his men up, and without hesitation this one regiment charged across an open field into more than five times their number. The heroic charge stunned Wilcox's men and stopped the advance. The Alabamans regrouped, however, and slammed volleys into the 1st Minnesota. Wilcox, his brigade's momentum halted by the charge of the Minnesotans, saw Barksdale's brigade retreat and uncover his right flank. Unsupported, he decided to pull his men back. Only forty-seven men of the 1st Minnesota survived the charge alive and unwounded. Still fresh Confederates advanced toward the Union center. A brigade under Ambrose Wright marched virtually unopposed up onto Cemetery Ridge north of Wilcox's brigade and seemed on the verge of making the final breakthrough that would cut the Union army in two. They fought furiously to hold their position as what was left of Hancock's II Corps attacked them from Cemetery Hill and rallying men from the Union III Corps assailed them from the south. Finally, with all the other Confederate brigades pulling back and darkness closing in, Wright had to give up his thrust into the Union line and fall back to Seminary Ridge. Longstreet's assault on the Union left was

THE PEACH ORCHARD
JULY 2, 6:30 P.M.

The Confederate brigade under William Barksdale crashes into the Union III Corps' line where it formed a salient at the Peach Orchard. After fierce fighting among the peach trees, the Confederates would break through and begin the rout that would push the shattered III Corps all the way back to Cemetery Ridge. Culp's Hill rises on the left horizon. The view is looking northeast from the southern part of Seminary Ridge.

over. His men had blown apart the Union III Corps, inflicting nine thousand casualties while taking six thousand. They had come close to first flanking and then piercing the Union line. But they had come up just short of realizing Lee's vision of destroying the Union army that day.

Another opportunity to tear apart the Army of the Potomac was presenting itself on the eastern slopes of Culp's Hill. Lee's plan had called for Ewell's II Corps to make a demonstration against the Union right flank to ensure that no reinforcements could be sent from there to interfere with Longstreet's assault. In this Ewell had failed by attacking too late. In fact, when things had looked their worst for the Union and Meade had watched Sickles's corps come streaming back in a rout, he had sent word for Slocum's XII Corps to abandon Culp's Hill and march southwest to shore up the Union left. On getting the word, Slocum could not believe he should give up his portion of the heights and leave the entire right flank of the Union army to be held only by the beaten and unreliable XI Corps, now arrayed on the northern part of Cemetery Hill. Meade allowed him to leave one brigade behind, but ordered him to move the rest of his corps as quickly as possible southwest. This Slocum did, leaving behind a brigade under George Greene to hold all of Culp's Hill. Meade's panicked call to practically abandon Culp's Hill to support his left went out too late to play any role in stopping Longstreet's attack. The one XII Corps division under Thomas Ruger that did arrive on the west slope of Cemetery Ridge were too late to take part in the battle, and the other under John Geary got lost en route and never made it at all. All that Meade's orders had accomplished was to give Ewell and his II Corps an unexpected opportunity to break the Union right. Shortly after 6 P.M., with only the fourteen hundred men of Greene's brigade left to defend Culp's Hill, Ewell launched his attack. This was not going to be a demonstration to keep the Federals pinned down. Ewell was sending in everything he had—at least that was the plan. Johnson's division would assault Culp's Hill from the northeast while Ewell's other two divisions, under Early and Rodes, would attack Cemetery Hill from the north and northwest. Johnson's division went in first and banged into the stout breastworks containing Greene's brigade, just down from the crest of Culp's Hill. The fire coming from the shielded Yankees pinned hundreds of Rebels behind trees and rocks on the northeast slopes. Johnson's line contained six thousand men, however, and they soon overlapped Greene's line to the south where the rest of the XII Corps' defensive works lay abandoned. Greene pulled his men back to a last line of defense surrounding the crest of Culp's Hill and prayed for help before he ran out of men or ammunition.

By this time Early's division had started their attack on the XI Corps holding east Cemetery Hill. These were the same men they had whipped the day before northeast of Gettysburg. The attack was centered on a large brick gate, the entrance to Evergreen Cemetery from which the hill got its name. Just below the gate a line of Federal artillery aimed downhill at the advancing Rebels. These artillerymen had been firing on Ewell's corps all day, and the Rebel soldiers couldn't wait to come to grips with them. Early sent in two brigades, one from North Carolina under Isaac Avery and the other Louisianans under Harry Hays, to begin the assault. He held back a third under Gordon to support any breakthrough. The Rebels climbed the hill in long lines, holding formation and pushing the Federal infantry all the way back to the guns. The Federal cannon fired canister from close range, tearing out ghastly holes in the gray lines, but Early's men closed ranks and came on with a rush. They fought hand-to-hand amid the Federal cannon, clubbing and bayoneting their daylong antagonists. The surviving men of the XI Corps and the Union artillerymen finally abandoned the guns and retreated west through the cemetery. Early's

THE CHARGE OF THE 1ST MINNESOTA JULY 2, 7:15 P.M.

The rout of the III Corps left an undefended gap in the Union line on the lower slopes of Cemetery Ridge. A fresh Confederate brigade of Alabamans was marching in to assault that gap and split the Union line in two. General Winfield Hancock ordered the 1st Minnesota Regiment to charge the Alabamans and buy him time to bring in reinforcements. The 262 men from Minnesota charged five times their number and gave Hancock the time he needed. Only 47 men of the 1st Minnesota survived the charge alive and unhurt. The view is looking southwest from Cemetery Ridge.

men captured the cannon and gained the crest of Cemetery Hill. Once again the Army of Northern Virginia had pierced the Federal line. This time there was support close at hand. Early had Gordon's brigade ready, and Rodes's entire division still had not been committed. They never would be. Early saw his men gain the heights, but held back Gordon's brigade because he did not see Rodes's division attacking on his right. Rodes, having paid heavily for flinging in his division without preparation the day before, had taken longer than expected to assemble his men in Gettysburg for the attack and was late in getting started. Early hesitated. If he sent in Gordon's brigade he would have no reserve. Without support from Rodes, committing Gordon would leave this part of the line defenseless if his division was repulsed. Early held Gordon's brigade back. The two brigades on the crest of Cemetery Hill looked for support that never came. What did come was a Federal counterattack by portions of the XI Corps sent from the northwest slope of Cemetery Hill that should have been under attack by Rodes's division. It was so dark by this time that Avery's and Hays's brigades, holding the captured guns at the top of the hill, could not make out whether the troops approaching from the northwest were Yankee or Rebel. They held their fire. They were expecting support from Rodes's division from that quarter and only became aware of their mistake when a short-range volley erupted in their faces from the shadowy figures to their front. More blue troops arrived from the southwest, and the pocket of gray soldiers holding the crest began to contract and fall back. With no support coming in and the Union numbers mounting, the two Confederate brigades had to escape back through the darkness, leaving the captured guns and another chance for victory behind. By the time Rodes had his division ready to attack north of Cemetery Hill, it was full dark and Early's division was pulling off the heights. Realizing he was too late, Rodes canceled his attack entirely. It was another bad day at Gettysburg for Robert Rodes.

The darkness was also playing havoc with Johnson's attack on Culp's Hill. The Rebels had occupied the abandoned Union lines on the south slope of the hill, but Greene's men were still holding the crest. Struggling in the dark to shift the attack to the north to assault the heights caused confusion and some serious mistakes. More than once a Confederate regiment fired into oncoming soldiers only to find that they were slaughtering their own troops. By the time they had sorted themselves out for a final attack to take the hill, Yankee reinforcements were coming in. Most of them were from Slocum's XII Corps, who had

The gatehouse of Evergreen Cemetery stood behind the Union lines on Cemetery Hill. This postbattle photograph shows the earthworks thrown up to protect Federal artillery positions.

Late in the day of July 2, two Confederate brigades from Jubal Early's division assault the Union line on the northeast slope of Cemetery Ridge in front of the brick gatehouse. The Rebel assault would break the line and reach the crest of the hill. The view is looking southeast from the northern slope of Cemetery Ridge.

This 1863 photograph shows the Federal artillery positions on Cemetery Hill that were overrun during the early-evening attack. Culp's Hill can be seen rising in the background.

finally turned around from their pointless marching and were arriving back to reclaim their lines. Coming in cloaked in darkness, the arrival of the XII Corps prompted a series of vicious close-range firefights; no one knew friend or foe until they were almost on top of each other. This kind of confused fighting went on late into the night, ending with the Federals still holding Culp's Hill and reoccupying some of the uphill trenches on the southern shoulder. Johnson's men clung to the trenches down the slope and waited until morning.

Even before the fighting had ended on the slopes of Culp's Hill, George Meade called his corps commanders together at his headquarters in the Leister House on Cemetery Hill to discuss what the Army of the Potomac should do next. Meade had worked furiously throughout the afternoon to find and send reinforcements to shore up his threatened line, on first the left and then the right flank. Several times throughout the day he had seen his army come close to disaster, and he was not at all sure it could survive another day like the one it had just been through. Still, the army was intact and had been bolstered late in the day by the arrival of John Sedgwick's VI Corps, making up for most of the day's losses. Dan Sickles's unfortunate salient had been crushed, but this had only brought the Union line back to Cemetery Ridge and the Round Tops where Meade had wanted it in the first place. Meade and his commanders conferred for three hours while the firing died down on hills to the east. In the end it was decided that the army should stay in position and fight it out. The Rebel incursion on the south slopes of Culp's Hill would have to be dealt with first thing in the morning. After that, the army would remain on the defensive and, once again, see what Robert E. Lee would do.

Lee had spent the day on Seminary Ridge trying to see the progress of his attack through the smoke and trees. He had issued the orders for the attack at around 10 A.M. and, other than urging Longstreet to get started at noon, spent the rest of the day waiting for and watching the assault. As was his way, he let his subordinates carry out his plans and did not interfere once his orders had been issued. Lee had seen the shattering of Sickles's III Corps and had watched as the attack had rolled up to and finally been beaten back from Cemetery Ridge. He also had received reports of the actions on Culp's and Cemetery Hills. He was disappointed with the results. He realized how close the Army of Northern Virginia had come to victory and felt that a lack of coordination among his commanders had caused the attacks to come up just short. This failure in coordination caused the

An 1880s photograph of the same area taken from an observation tower.

brigades that pierced the Union line to go unsupported. Lee was determined to continue the attack the next day and just as determined that the attack would be done in a way that there would be no failure in coordination or support. He had in mind a huge concentrated blow at a single point in the Union line. He would spend the night planning which troops to use and where they would strike.

At least Lee would have his entire army on the field to finish the battle. Longstreet's third division under George Pickett had marched in from the west, too late to take part in the day's fighting. Also arriving, finally, were Jeb Stuart and his wayward cavalry. Stuart and his men had continued north after capturing the wagon train near Washington and spent the next few days desperately trying to rejoin Lee's army. They had clashed with Union cavalry and militia en route, and by the time they reached Carlisle, twenty-eight miles north of Gettysburg, the troopers and horses were completely exhausted. Stuart's glorious ride had turned into a sleepless weeklong nightmare that accomplished little other than wearing out good horses and men. Stuart finally learned that a battle was in progress at Gettysburg and rode in ahead of his straggling column. Lee, whose relationship with his young cavalry commander had always been jovial, greeted Stuart icily and sent him away with orders to rest his troopers. He would have plenty of work for them tomorrow.

The second day of battle at Gettysburg was over. Lee's men had attacked both the left and right flanks of the Union line and come close to scoring the breakthrough Lee was hoping for. In the end, though, Meade's blue line had held. Both armies had fought desperately, and the sacrifices were enormous. Twenty-eight thousand men had been killed or wounded in the fighting around Gettysburg in the two days of battle, more mangled men than in any battle so far in the war. Only darkness had stopped the killing. The exhausted armies knew they would have more slaughter to endure when the sun came up on July 3.

DAY THREE *July 3, 1863*

Some of the slaughter did not wait for the sun to rise. The Rebel incursion into the entrenchments on the lower slopes of Culp's Hill threatened the whole Union position, and General Slocum assigned Alpheus "Old Pap" Williams, his senior division commander, the task of leading the XII Corps to drive them out. By four o'clock in the morning, "Old Pap" had brought up all the artillery he could bring to bear on the men of Johnson's Rebel division down the hill and unleashed a barrage that signaled the start of another hot day of battle. Johnson's men had received no change in orders since the night before and were preparing to continue the assault on the crest of Culp's Hill when the cannon fire rained

BOMBARDMENT AND MEADE'S HEADQUARTERS JULY 3, 1 P.M.

The first shells from the 150-gun Confederate barrage begin to explode on the back, or eastern slope of Cemetery Ridge. Most of the Rebel artillery was aimed just a bit too high, and the shells did the most damage behind the Union main line. Meade's headquarters in the Leister House, the small white building in the distance, took several hits and forced Meade and his staff to flee east to safety. The view is looking southeast from the top of Cemetery Hill.

An 1863 photograph of the Leister House, which served as General Meade's headquarters during the second and third days of the battle.

down upon them. With no artillery support of their own, they threw themselves up the hill, dodging behind shattering rocks and splintering trees. Waves of rifle fire shot out from the Union breastworks, heightening the maddening chorus of sound that made it impossible to hear an order even if it was shouted next to an ear. The uphill attack came to a halt as nothing could live long in the open in front of the XII Corps' lines. Unable to advance and unwilling to retreat, Johnson's men took up positions behind stout trees and rocky outcroppings and blasted away uphill into the thick smoke. The rain of lead passing between the lines was like nothing the soldiers on either side had ever witnessed. Large trees were splintered by repeated hits until they came crashing down among the soldiers. Several times the Rebel lines surged forward in doomed charges that left dead and wounded men piled in front of the Union breastworks. Finally word came to the fought-out Rebels to pull back. Johnson had received orders from General Ewell to call off the attack. Ewell had heard from General Lee.

Lee awoke on Seminary Ridge after a few short hours of sleep and soon heard the distant rumble of battle over on the eastern hills. Already his plan to coordinate his attacks for that day was going awry. The plan of attack he would finalize that morning was to make a huge assault on the center of the Union line on Cemetery Hill from the west while Ewell's corps attacked Culp's Hill from the east hard enough to keep any Union forces there pinned down. There would be no echelon attack this time. After a massive artillery bombardment, they would all go in together in what Lee hoped would be an overwhelming blow that would split the Union army in half. General Longstreet would again command the main attack, but only the five thousand men in Pickett's fresh division from Longstreet's corps would participate. Longstreet's other two divisions, Hood's and McLaws's, had been too badly mauled the previous day to take part. Lee would have to piece together the rest of the assault force from any brigades who hadn't been heavily engaged the day before. Heth's division, who had done so much hard fighting on McPherson's Ridge on the first day, were now rested and would join the assault to the left of Pickett's division. Heth was down with a head wound, so they would be led in by Brigadier General James Johnston Pettigrew. Two more brigades under Isaac Trimble would join Pettigrew's men in the assault. Two additional brigades were culled from Anderson's division to bolster Pickett's three brigades on the right. All told, close to fifteen thousand men would form along the eastern slopes of Seminary Ridge to assault what was left of Hancock's II Corps waiting almost a mile away behind a stone wall on Cemetery Ridge. A little copse of trees, no more than overgrown brush really, stood out along the dawn skyline in the middle of Hancock's line as Lee looked out across the fields that separated the armies. He ordered that the forces under Pickett and Pettigrew should converge on those trees for the final assault into the Union lines.

Gathering all those brigades and the 150 artillery pieces that would soften up the Union lines in preparation for the assault would take time. Lee sent orders to Ewell to hold off on his attack on Culp's Hill until later in the day. By the time Lee's messenger reached Ewell, it was already far too late. Ewell's men were spending themselves against the Union breastworks on the eastern slopes of Culp's Hill before Lee could stop them. The opportunity to pin part of the Union army down away from Cemetery Hill had been lost. The attack from Seminary Ridge would have to be enough.

The man who would lead the assault did not think it would be enough. Longstreet had seen two of his divisions smash themselves up against the Union defenses the day before, and while they had come tantalizingly close to cracking the Union line, the horrendous casualties they suffered practically wrecked them. The Union position atop Cemetery Ridge, protected by a stout stone wall and bristling with troops and cannon, reminded him of a position his own men had once held on Marye's Heights overlooking Fredericksburg. The Union assault on his line that day could hardly be described as a battle. It was simply murder. The Federal lines marched up to within a few hundred yards of the wall and were mown down, regiment after regiment, by Longstreet's men.

A photograph taken just days after the battle from the Taneytown Road looking north shows the Leister House and Farm and the damage caused by the Confederate bombardment that preceded Pickett's Charge.

Now Longstreet had to order his own men toward a similar wall. When he met with General Lee that morning, he appealed once again to his commander to cancel the attack and move the army south and east to get between Meade and Washington. Lee again waved him off. He had come north to destroy the Union army. He had smashed in both its flanks the day before. Today he would send an irresistible force against its center. In his mind, nothing could stop a coordinated assault by fifteen thousand soldiers from the Army of Northern Virginia. The cost would undoubtedly be high, but once his men had pierced the Union line and sent the Army of the Potomac reeling back, Stuart's troopers were all now on hand to follow up and destroy the remnants as they retreated toward Washington. It was the kind of all-or-nothing gamble that had made Lee a legend. The assault would go on. Lee ordered Longstreet to gather the agreed-upon forces in the trees along Seminary Ridge. He also sent word to Stuart to prepare his recovering cavalry for action. Stuart was to take his troopers out the York Road east of Gettysburg and get them in position to pounce on what Lee hoped would be a panicked Federal retreat later in the day.

A key part of Lee's plan was an enormous bombardment of the center of the Union line by every piece of artillery available. Lee hoped that such a huge cannonade, unlike anything ever seen before in the war, would smash the enemy's artillery on the heights and kill, maim, or terrorize most of the Union infantry his attacking force would have to face. Lee gave much of the responsibility for placing the more than 150 cannon that would participate in the bombardment to twenty-eight-year-old Colonel E. Porter Alexander. Alexander spent much of the morning of July 3 positioning the guns in a giant shallow arc that ran from just east of the Lutheran seminary, down south along Seminary Ridge, ending just east of the Peach Orchard. The gun crews and horses, dragging cannon and caissons loaded with ammunition, worked furiously to get in position through the morning as regiment after regiment of

Confederate soldiers filed into the trees behind Seminary Ridge. The day had become hot, and the thousands of ragged Rebel infantry who would soon be called upon to decide the battle and perhaps the course of the war enjoyed a brief respite in the leafy shade along the ridge.

George Meade, holed up with his staff in the small white Leister House that served as his headquarters—a few hundred yards east of the Copse of Trees Lee had pointed to earlier that morning—was working furiously on the final details of his army's defensive alignment as the day drifted past noon. The morning had gone well for the Union commander. The dangerous Rebel hold on the lower slopes of Culp's Hill had been blasted back by "Old Pap" Williams's artillery and the XII Corps. Both of his army's flanks that had come so close to crumbling the day before had been reinforced and fortified during the night, including the Round Tops to the south. Meade had done all he could think of to prepare for what was to come. He was well aware, though, that Robert E. Lee had a way of upsetting even the best-laid plans. Reports had been arriving at his headquarters all morning of Rebel artillery moving in droves and positioning all along the eastern tree line of Seminary Ridge. Dust clouds kicked up by thousands of marching feet had been observed lingering above the hills off to the west. Lee was up to something and Meade, less than a week in command and already having seen his army suffer casualties too awful to contemplate, could only wait and react.

He didn't have to wait long. A growling rumble of sound from the southwest stopped Meade and his staff in the midst of their paperwork. The sound moved north and grew louder until it seemed as if the land off to the west were tearing itself open in a violent ripping quake. A cannonball came crashing through the wall of the crowded headquarters; another splintered through the roof. Meade and his staff rushed toward the door just as a bounding iron ball tore through the row of horses tethered outside, gutting and dismembering the

PICKETT'S CHARGE

JULY 3, 3:15 P.M.

The Confederate battle lines re-form after struggling over the rail fences that bordered the Emmitsburg Road before beginning their final assault on the Union line. Union artillery from Cemetery Ridge and Little Round Top took a devastating toll during the mile-long Rebel advance. The view is looking west toward Seminary Ridge from just inside the Union line on Cemetery Ridge.

shrieking mounts. Meade was hustled off east away from the growing rain of metal that was turning the crest of Cemetery Hill into chaos. Lee's bombardment had begun.

The huge Confederate cannonade began around one o'clock in the afternoon. Starting with the batteries down near the Peach Orchard and rolling one after another north along Seminary Ridge, the guns spewed flame and thick white smoke, sending tons of metal screaming across the fields toward Cemetery Hill. Those who witnessed the lethal eruption never could quite describe the noise it made. It was simply the loudest thing they had ever heard, times ten. The impact of all that exploding metal on the few acres of ground atop Cemetery Hill sent Meade and every other soldier in blue diving for cover. The infantry on the front line pressed themselves into the stone wall as the ground exploded around them. The soldiers, teamsters, and cavalry on the eastern back slope of Cemetery Ridge, who had thought themselves shielded from danger by the high ground, suddenly found themselves in the middle of the worst of the maelstrom. The Confederate gunners were aiming for the infantry and artillery on the front line, but many of the shots were just slightly high, sending the shells scything down the back of the hill at a shallow angle certain to hit something on the way through. What they hit were men, horses, wagons, and caissons loaded with ammunition. The resulting mayhem was catastrophic for those in the crowded rear area, but did not have near the same effect on the Union front-line troops after the initial salvos. The Confederate aim got worse as the thick smoke obscured their view of the hill entirely. The Army of the Potomac had plenty of artillery that was quick to respond. More than eighty Union guns lined up on the hill, down the ridge, and even on the crest of Little Round Top soon were firing back at the exposed Rebel gunners. The fields between the lines were soon entirely blanketed with thick white smoke as hundreds of cannon on both sides fired almost blind. The Union guns also tended to overshoot their targets, but instead of slaughtering rear-area personnel the high Federal rounds landed squarely in the midst of the gray infantry preparing for the assault behind their artillery. The tree limbs above them that had been providing welcome shade suddenly turned into lethal splinters as hot iron balls crashed through. Longstreet's attack force took hundreds of casualties before they could even get started.

The artillery duel continued for almost two hours until many of the Union officers realized they were using up ammunition at an alarming rate. The field was so obscured by smoke that their counterfire was accomplishing very little as far as they could tell. It was obvious to everyone by then that such a bombardment had to be the prelude to a large-scale attack. Many of the Federal batteries stopped firing to husband their ammunition and wait for the much better targets that were sure to come. The slackening Union artillery fire did not go unnoticed by Colonel Alexander. He interpreted the meager return fire as a sign that his guns had knocked out much of the Union artillery defending the opposing ridgeline. He sent word to General Longstreet. If the attack was to be made, it had better start while his guns still had a few rounds to support the assault.

General George Pickett was waiting and watching the artillery bombardment along with Longstreet at the edge of the trees on Seminary Ridge. The Virginia-born Pickett had resigned as a captain in the Federal army when the war started and had risen to command a division in the Army of Northern Virginia. Last in his class at West Point, Pickett was almost childishly vain, cut from much the same cloth as Jeb Stuart. He wore his hair in perfumed ringlets and was given to romantic ramblings about his teenage sweetheart. While he and his men had participated in several major battles in the war, the glory and acclaim he so desired had thus far eluded him. The first two days of battle at Gettysburg had been fought without him and his men and he yearned for a chance to write his name into history on the third and climactic day. He would soon get his wish.

Longstreet stared into the smoky haze trying to make out the damage the bombardment was doing to the Union line. His gut told him that while the bombardment had been spectacular, the forces up on Cemetery Ridge still had not been broken up enough to make the assault a success. There were just too many blue soldiers in too strong a position. When the message came in from Alexander, Pickett approached Longstreet and asked for the order to start the attack. Longstreet hesitated. He couldn't bring himself to say the words and send thousands of the South's best soldiers to certain death. Pickett's blood was up, and he implored Longstreet to let them go. To wait any longer would give the Federals time to regroup after the bombardment and make things even worse. Finally, Longstreet could only bring himself to nod grimly at Pickett's appeals.

Pickett turned and shouted the orders, which carried all along Seminary Ridge. The attack had begun.

Out from the trees all along the east side of Seminary Ridge came the battle lines of brigade after brigade of Rebel troops, Pickett's force to the south and Pettigrew's men to the north. A hundred yards out from the trees they stopped to dress their lines. Half a mile away across the undulating fields the Union infantry peered through the drifting smoke and saw a sight that made their hearts leap. Row after row of thousands of battle-hardened gray soldiers stood for a few moments in perfect parade-ground formation, colorful regimental flags fluttering in the breeze. It was a spectacular tableau that would crystallize forever in the minds of the men who witnessed it. Then the order to go forward was given and the huge assault force stepped off to close on the Union soldiers behind their rock wall. Guiding on their officers, the Confederates marched out at an even pace, struggling to maintain their lines as they crossed plowed fields and tore down rail fences. The Union artillery on the ridge had rushed to resupply their ammunition and replace any damaged batteries after the bombardment. Far from destroyed by the Rebel cannonade, the Federal guns soon began long-range fire at the packed Confederate battle lines. Shells began bursting in the midst of the formations, blasting bloody gaps in the brigades. Cannonballs bounded along through the lines, taking down whole rows of mangled men. Still the attack waves came forward, closing up the gaps and pushing halfway across the fields. On the left flank of the assault, one of Pettigrew's brigades—taking particularly heavy casualties from the guns posted near Ziegler's Grove on the far northwest slope of Cemetery Hill—was surprised by a close-range rifle volley. The 8th Ohio Regiment, posted out in front of the Union lines as skirmishers, rose up out of tall grass and blasted the Rebel flank as it passed. This proved too much; the battered gray brigade broke and ran to the rear. The rows of marching men to their right instinctively moved away from the devastating flanking fire, causing the Rebel advance to bunch up toward the center. The same kind of slaughter was taking place on the right flank of the assault. The Union batteries atop Little Round Top were plunging fire directly down into that flank and tearing apart whole regiments. As on the left, Pickett's men moved away from this fire, and the southern brigades began to tangle up in the center as they approached the Emmitsburg Road. The rail fences along the road caused more confusion as the sweating, blood-spattered men struggled to tear down or climb over the barriers. Three Pennsylvania regiments under Hancock, around six thousand men in all, waited behind the low stone wall astride the Copse of Trees that was the focus of the attack. As the desperate southern soldiers pushed across the road, the Pennsylvanians let loose their first volley, knocking down hundreds of Confederates. Yankee cannon had been pushed right up to the wall, and these joined in with canister fire, sending hundreds of small metal balls tearing through the clustered Rebel ranks. The assaulting force seemed to recoil away from the fiery stone wall, but soon rallied and came on again. The Rebels fired back through the smoke

ASSAULTING THE WALL

JULY 3, 3:30 P.M.

The Rebel assault force under General James Pettigrew closes on the wall protecting Cemetery Ridge north of The Angle. The final Confederate surge on this section of the Union line would reach the wall only to be blasted back by close-range rifle volleys and canister shot. The view is looking south from a hundred yards north of The Angle.

and rushed forward to close on the wall. Union gunners and infantry along the wall began to fall under the southern onslaught. Just north of the Copse of Trees, the rock wall protecting the Union line turned sharply east for fifty yards before turning north again. This created a salient in the Union line that bore the brunt of the southern fire as the men guarding this corner, forever after known as The Angle, were exposed to a withering flanking fire from the Rebels passing to the north. The Union ranks began to waver. Still, the protected blue infantry were giving out far more damage than they were taking. The murderous Union fire had by then stripped the attacking force of thousands of men and all of its general officers except Lewis Armistead. General Armistead, an old friend of Hancock from before the war, rallied about a thousand men for a final rush toward the Union line just south of The Angle. The gray soldiers fell in heaps during the desperate charge, but Armistead and a few hundred men managed to reach the wall and force the blue line to collapse back. Leaping the wall, Armistead and his men surged forward. For a moment it seemed that they had done it—pierced the Union line to send Hancock's corps and finally the whole Army of the Potomac into retreat. It was only for a moment, though. Too few men had broken the line with Armistead, and thousands of Federal soldiers were close at hand to patch the break. Hancock himself, riding behind the lines, directed reinforcements forward to push back the Rebels. Armistead was mortally wounded as he reached out his hand for a Federal cannon barrel and his dwindling command collapsed around him. Tradition would hold that where he fell marked the "High Water Mark of the Confederacy." Of the men who had followed Armistead through the line, those who could broke for the rear and leapt back over the wall. Many more, surrounded by Union soldiers, were shot down or forced to surrender. The entire Confederate attack was by then breaking up and pulling back all along the front of the wall. A Vermont brigade positioned south of the fighting marched out from their line and fired devastating volleys into right flank of the massed Rebels, turning the Confederate retreat into a rout. General Pickett, having watched the repulse from the Cordori House along the Emmitsburg Road, joined the remnants of his command as they stumbled back toward Seminary Ridge. The failed attack would forever carry his name: Pickett's Charge. More than seven thousand men, the cream of the Army of Northern Virginia, never made it back to their lines. General Lee rode out to meet his battered army as they struggled back to the ridge. "Everything will be all right," he told them. "All this has been my fault." When he met Pickett riding back, he told him to prepare his division for a Union counterattack Lee was sure would come. Pickett could only reply that he had no division left.

All along Cemetery Ridge, the northern soldiers raised a loud husky cheer as they saw the Confederates retreat back across the fields. General Meade, having spent the battle in the rear, rode to the front just as the last of the Rebels drifted out of range. Several of his officers urged him to attack Seminary Ridge immediately. They felt that the crippled Army of Northern Virginia could be finished off by a massive Federal assault. Once again, Meade chose to be cautious. His own army had been badly hurt by the bombardment and brutal Confederate charge. The hundreds of dead and wounded Union soldiers along the wall were enough to convince Meade that a hurried counterattack could be disastrous. Lee had just shattered a large part of his army against Cemetery Ridge. Meade feared similar results if he sent his own men across those same torn fields. The Army of the Potomac had done enough for that day.

The repulse of Pickett's Charge and the appalling casualties it inflicted on the Army of Northern Virginia would end Lee's dream of destroying the Army of the Potomac and marching on Washington. Now he would turn his attention to preparing his men to resist any Union counterattack while turning his army back toward Virginia. That night, while

THE ANGLE
JULY 3, 3:40 P.M.

In the final act of Pickett's Charge, a few hundred Confederates led by General Lewis Armistead break the Union line between the Copse of Trees and The Angle. This final Rebel thrust marked the High Water Mark of the Confederacy and threatened to split the Union army. The break-through could not be supported by the rest of the shattered Rebel assault force, however, and Armistead was soon mortally wounded and his men shot down or captured by the rallying men of Hancock's II Corps. The view is looking west from just east of The Angle. The tree line of Seminary Ridge marks the horizon. General Pickett is believed to have watched the assualt from the Codori House, which can be seen through the smoke on the left.

This 1880s photograph shows the Copse of Trees that was the focal point of Pickett's Charge. Big Round Top can be seen rising in the distance on the left.

Lee pulled back all three Confederate corps to Seminary Ridge, word came in that Stuart's cavalry had engaged in a savage fight west of Gettysburg at just about the same time Longstreet's men were assaulting the Union wall. Stuart had tried to slice into the Federal rear that afternoon but had been stopped by determined Union cavalry, including a Michigan brigade led by twenty-three-year-old George Armstrong Custer. Now all Stuart and his troopers could do was try to cover the long retreat of Lee's army back to Virginia, a retreat the would be even harder to endure because of news that would come in from the West. The next day, the siege of Vicksburg would end in a Confederate surrender. Ulysses S. Grant and his army had torn the Confederacy in half and opened the entire Mississippi River to Union control.

The next day, July 4, 1863, would be spent by both armies gathering up the wounded and resting after the exhausting three-day battle. The battle had cost the Army of Northern Virginia twenty-eight thousand casualties and the Army of the Potomac twenty-three thousand in killed, wounded, and missing. Lee would keep his infantry in position throughout the day while he started his long wagon train back through the South Mountain passes toward the Potomac River. The wagons of the seventeen-mile train were piled with wounded men who had to endure a long, painful trip along the rutted roads out of Pennsylvania and across Maryland. That afternoon the sky opened up and a downpour washed the blood from the thousands of torn bodies still strewn over the fields and in the woods around Gettysburg.

Lee started the rest of his army on its way home under cover of darkness that night. He had lost a third of his men during the battle, and the survivors were still deep in enemy country. George Meade, spurred on by telegrams from Lincoln and Halleck in Washington, would start a cautious pursuit the next day when he found the Rebel lines abandoned along

Seminary Ridge. The Army of Northern Virginia would win the race to the river crossing, only to find their way blocked by the swollen Potomac. What had been a tranquil, easily forded river on the way north had been turned by the rain into a raging torrent that barred any escape. Lee did the only thing he could as the Union army closed in. He had his men prepare a defensive ring around the river crossing and waited for Meade to attack.

Meade was determined to do just that. He had attempted to cut Lee's army off from reaching the Potomac, but having failed in that he now saw an opportunity to crush it while it was pinned against a swollen river. Meade was still careful not to rush his tired army into a disaster, despite the urgent pleas from Washington not to allow Lee to escape. He had lost a fourth of his army at Gettysburg, and while he still had more than seventy thousand men to hurl at the Army of Northern Virginia, the fifty thousand remaining Confederates were now solidly dug in and ready. It would take a few days for Meade to position his army for an assault. In those few days the river began to fall, and Lee's engineers were able to jury-rig a pontoon bridge to the far shore. On July 13 the Army of Northern Virginia started to cross back into Virginia. By the next morning, when Meade's assault was planned to start, only a small rear guard was left on the Maryland shore. In the final melee to get the last of Lee's army over the bridge, the Federal soldiers scooped up a few hundred prisoners and mortally wounded General James Johnston Pettigrew, the commander of the left wing of Pickett's Charge.

The Gettysburg Campaign was over. Lee had managed to keep his ravaged army intact and get most of it safely back to Virginia soil. Because he did, the war would go on for two more even bloodier years. Lee would use the troops he brought back as the core of the army that defended Richmond until the final collapse in 1865. Never again would the Army of Northern Virginia have the strength to seriously threaten the North with invasion.

A companion photograph from the 1880s shows the stone wall defended by Hancock's II Corps just south of The Angle. The Codori House and Emmitsburg Road can be seen in the distance.

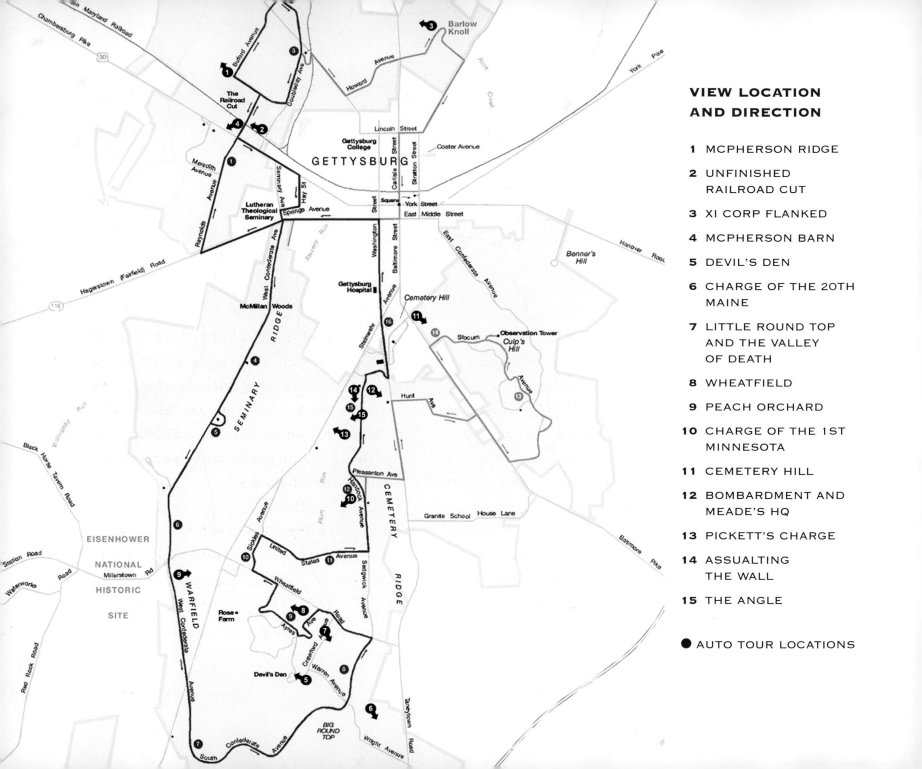

VIEW LOCATION AND DIRECTION

1 MCPHERSON RIDGE

2 UNFINISHED RAILROAD CUT

3 XI CORP FLANKED

4 MCPHERSON BARN

5 DEVIL'S DEN

6 CHARGE OF THE 20TH MAINE

7 LITTLE ROUND TOP AND THE VALLEY OF DEATH

8 WHEATFIELD

9 PEACH ORCHARD

10 CHARGE OF THE 1ST MINNESOTA

11 CEMETERY HILL

12 BOMBARDMENT AND MEADE'S HQ

13 PICKETT'S CHARGE

14 ASSUALTING THE WALL

15 THE ANGLE

● AUTO TOUR LOCATIONS

TOURING THE BATTLEFIELD WITH THIS BOOK

The National Park Service has created an automobile tour of Gettysburg National Military Park with sixteen stops at locations of interest. This tour is a great way to navigate the park and get an overview of the battle from the information provided at each stop. Readers of *Gettysburg: You Are There* who visit the battlefield can add to their enjoyment of both the park and the book by finding the locations along the tour that correspond with the battle scenes presented here. The locations for the battle scenes are along the marked tour route and can be found on the map provided.

MCPHERSON RIDGE This view looks to the west northwest, where Buford Avenue turns north toward Oak Hill. A service road continues west and is used in the battle scene to simulate the Chambersburg Pike, now a modern highway. Herr's Ridge can be seen to the west, and the course of Willoughby Run can be seen at the bottom of the valley marked by trees on its banks.

THE UNFINISHED RAILROAD CUT This view looks west from the north bank of the Railroad Cut just east of the modern bridge and shows the deepest section of the cut. No bridge or railroad tracks existed at the time of the battle. It is easy to see how the men of Davis's Rebel brigade made the mistake of marching into a trap. The shallow section of the cut to the west made a perfect trench to fire from. Only when it deepened did it become indefensible.

THE FLANKING OF THE IX CORPS This view is from Barlow's Knoll looking west northwest toward Oak Hill. As with most of the battle scenes, there were far fewer trees in this area in 1863. The actual battle line of the XI Corps would have been a few hundred yards to the south of the position they occupy in the scene.

MCPHERSON BARN This view looks southwest from the south end of the bridge crossing the Railroad Cut. The barn is very well preserved but the rest of the farm, including the McPherson family home and an outbuilding, no longer exists. The distinctively shaped outbuilding was re-created in the battle scene using a similar building, which still exists, at the Culp Farm in eastern Gettysburg.

DEVIL'S DEN This view looks west from the parking area just east of Devil's Den. During the battle this area was filled with boulders that were removed to create the park road. The large trees that now cover the top of Houck's Ridge didn't exist in 1863 and were removed in the battle scene.

THE CHARGE OF THE 20TH MAINE This view looks southeast from the line defended by the 20th Maine on the wooded southern slope of Little Round Top. While the Maine men would have piled some rocks up into hastily constructed breastworks before they were attacked, they did not have time build the stone wall that exists at the location now and is included in the battle scene.

LITTLE ROUND TOP AND THE VALLEY OF DEATH This view looks southeast across Plum Run toward Little Round Top from the top of the northern end of Houck's Ridge. It is hard to believe that such a natural defensive position was virtually ignored by the Union army until almost too late on the second day of battle. The monuments atop Little Round Top and the park road through the valley were removed from the battle scene.

THE WHEATFIELD This view looks west from the eastern edge of the Wheatfield north of the park road. The trees on the far side of the field were much less abundant in 1863 than in the battle scene.

THE PEACH ORCHARD This view is from the top of the Longstreet Tower on Confederate Avenue looking east-northeast. The height of the tower makes it an excellent vantage point to take in the entire panorama of the battlefield. The Peach Orchard covered a larger area in 1863 than it does today and in the battle scene.

THE CHARGE OF THE 1ST MINNESOTA This view looks southwest toward the Trostle Farm from the monument to the 1st Minnesota located on Hancock Avenue. The ground between this location and the Peach Orchard was much less densely wooded in 1863.

CEMETERY HILL This view is from Cemetery Hill looking southeast along the Baltimore Pike. Some roads and large modern buildings have been removed from the battle scene. The distinctive Evergreen Cemetery gate has been moved about a hundred yards southeast of its actual location to be included in the scene.

BOMBARDMENT AND MEADE'S HEADQUARTERS This view is looking southeast from the field north of the pathway to the Leister House on the back slope of Cemetery Ridge. It is easy to see why the soldiers in the area felt shielded from danger until the first shells began to rain down during Lee's preattack bombardment.

PICKETT'S CHARGE This view is from behind the stone wall between The Angle and the Copse of Trees, looking west toward Seminary Ridge. From this location, the distance covered by the Confederate lines of battle during the charge can be appreciated.

ASSAULTING THE WALL This view looks south along the Cemetery Ridge stone wall just north of The Angle. Standing at this location will give the visitor some idea of how exposed the Confederate soldiers must have felt while closing on the Federal lines behind the wall.

THE ANGLE This view looks southwest from point where the stone wall turns north from The Angle. The location gives a good sense of why the Union soldiers occupying The Angle found themselves exposed to fire from two sides. Trees and monuments have been removed for the battle scene.

CREATING THESE IMAGES

*T*he battle images contained in this book are the result of my long-held desire to bring to life the brutal three-day struggle that has gone down in history as the battle of Gettysburg. Like many others, I've long felt a particular fascination with the collision of the Confederate Army of Northern Virginia with the Union Army of the Potomac in July 1863. The work of hundreds of writers has fueled my interest in the battle and the men who fought there. Their descriptions of the battle, and the terrain over which it was fought, left vivid images in my imagination. Advances in digital photography and digital imaging software in recent years have made it possible to re-create these mental images on paper.

The first step was to tour Gettysburg National Military Park and take photographs at the locations of the major events of the battle. Few, if any, historic places in America have as many well-known and dramatic features as the landscape around Gettysburg. Places like Devil's Den, Little Round Top, The Angle, McPherson Barn, and the Railroad Cut provide a visual feast for both the casual visitor and the serious historian. Once the location photographs were taken, they had to be modified to eliminate as many of the modern intrusions on the current day battlefield as possible. In the image titled *The Unfinished Railroad Cut,* for example, a modern automobile bridge that carries park traffic had to be removed, as did the railroad ties and tracks.

Once these modern distractions had been eliminated, the battle scene was created by combining hundreds of cropped photographs of Civil War reenactors, taken over several years and matched to the historical action. These soldiers had to be meticulously blended into the scenes using layering, shadowing, and cropping. Next came the addition of cannon, caissons, flags, smoke, and explosions where appropriate to give the image the look of a photograph taken at the time of the battle. Some of the images, like *The Charge of the 1st Minnesota,* hark back to the long tradition of military art that emphasizes the glory of battle over accuracy. Others, like *The Wheatfield,* stay closer to the true deadly nature of the conflict. All of them come from my educated imagination with the hope that they will enhance the reader's understanding and appreciation of the battle of Gettysburg.

2002 photograph.

Postbattle bridge and track removed.

Re-created battlefield image.

INDEX